ANCIENT EGYPT

THE HISTORY OF WEAPONS AND WARFARE

ANCIENT EGYPT

Other books in this series include:

Ancient Greece
Ancient Rome
The Civil War
The Middle Ages
The Native Americans

ANCIENT EGYPT

DON NARDO

LUCENT
BOOKS®

THOMSON
GALE

San Diego • Detroit • New York • San Francisco • Cleveland • New Haven, Conn. • Waterville, Maine • London • Munich

THOMSON
━━━✦━━━ ™
GALE

Cover image: A painting from the front panel of a chest found in King Tutankhamen's tomb depicting the massacre of the Nubians.

LIBRARY OF CONGRESS CATALOGING-IN-PUBLICATION DATA

Nardo, Don, 1947–
    Ancient Egypt / Don Nardo.
        p. cm. — (History of weapons and warfare)
Summary: Discusses the weapons used by the ancient Egyptians and their different means of warfare.
Includes bibliographical references and index.
    ISBN 1-59018-066-6 (hardback : alk. paper)
1. Military art and science—Egypt—Juvenile literature. 2. Military weapons—Egypt—Juvenile literature. 3. Egypt—History, Military—Juvenile literature. 4. Military history, Ancient—Juvenile literature. [1. Military art and science—Egypt. 2. Egypt—History, Military. 3. Egypt—History—To 332 B.C.] I. Title. II. Series.
U31 .N37 2003
355'.00932—dc21

932
N

2002000447

Printed in the United States of America

Contents

Foreword

The earliest battle about which any detailed information has survived took place in 1274 B.C. at Kadesh, in Syria, when the armies of the Egyptian and Hittite empires clashed. For this reason, modern historians devote a good deal of attention to Kadesh. Yet they know that this battle and the war of which it was a part were not the first fought by the Egyptians and their neighbors. Many other earlier conflicts are mentioned in ancient inscriptions found throughout the Near East and other regions, as from the dawn of recorded history city-states fought one another for political or economic dominance.

Moreover, it is likely that warfare long predated city-states and written records. Some scholars go so far as to suggest that the Cro-Magnons, the direct ancestors of modern humans, wiped out another early human group—the Neanderthals—in a prolonged and fateful conflict in the dim past. Even if this did not happen, it is likely that even the earliest humans engaged in conflicts and battles over territory and other factors. "Warfare is almost as old as man himself," writes renowned military historian John Keegan, "and reaches into the most secret places of the human heart, places where self dissolves rational purpose, where pride reigns, where emotion is paramount, where instinct is king."

Even after humans became "civilized," with cities, writing, and organized religion, the necessity of war was widely accepted. Most people saw it as the most natural means of defending territory, maintaining security, or settling disputes. A character in a dialogue by the fourth-century B.C. Greek thinker Plato declares:

> All men are always at war with one another. . . . For what men in general term peace is only a name; in reality, every city is in a natural state of war with every other, not indeed proclaimed by heralds, but everlasting. . . . No possessions or institutions are of any value to him who is defeated in battle; for all the good things of the conquered pass into the hands of the conquerors.

Considering the thousands of conflicts that have raged across the world since Plato's time, it would seem that war is an inevitable part of the human condition.

War not only remains an ever-present reality, it has also had undeniably crucial and far-reaching effects on human society and its development. As Keegan puts it, "History lessons remind us that the states in which we live . . . have come to us through conflict, often of the most bloodthirsty sort." Indeed, the world's first and oldest nation-state,

Egypt, was born out of a war between the two kingdoms that originally occupied the area; the modern nations of Europe rose from the wreckage of the sweeping barbarian invasions that destroyed the Roman Empire; and the United States was established by a bloody revolution between British colonists and their mother country.

Victory in these and other wars resulted from varying factors. Sometimes the side that possessed overwhelming numbers or the most persistence won; other times superior generalship and strategy played key roles. In many cases, the side with the most advanced and deadly weapons was victorious. In fact, the invention of increasingly lethal and devastating tools of war has largely driven the evolution of warfare, stimulating the development of new counter-weapons, strategies, and battlefield tactics. Among the major advances in ancient times were the composite bow, the war chariot, and the stone castle. Another was the Greek phalanx, a mass of close-packed spearman marching forward as a unit, devastating all before it. In medieval times, the stirrup made it easier for a rider to stay on his horse, increasing the effectiveness of cavalry charges. And a progression of late medieval and modern weapons—including cannons, handguns, rifles, submarines, airplanes, missiles, and the atomic bomb—made warfare deadlier than ever.

Each such technical advance made war more devastating and therefore more feared. And to some degree, people are drawn to and fascinated by what they fear, which accounts for the high level of interest in studies of warfare and the weapons used to wage it. Military historian John Hackett writes:

An inevitable result of the convergence of two tendencies, fear of war and interest in the past, has seen a thirst for more information about the making of war in earlier times, not only in terms of tools, techniques, and methods used in warfare, but also of the people by whom wars are and have been fought and how men have set about the business of preparing for and fighting them.

These themes—the evolution of warfare and weapons and how it has affected various human societies—lie at the core of the books in Lucent's History of Weapons and Warfare series. Each book examines the warfare of a pivotal people or era in detail, exploring the beliefs about and motivations for war at the time, as well as specifics about weapons, strategies, battle formations, infantry, cavalry, sieges, naval tactics, and the lives and experiences of both military leaders and ordinary soldiers. Where possible, descriptions of actual campaigns and battles are provided to illustrate how these various factors came together and decided the fate of city, a nation, or a people. Frequent quotations by contemporary participants or observers, as well as by noted modern military historians, add depth and authenticity. Each volume features an extensive annotated bibliography to guide those readers interested in further research to the most important and comprehensive works on warfare in the period in question. The series provides students and general readers with a useful means of understanding what is regrettably one of the driving forces of human history—violent human conflict.

Fighting to Keep the Dark Forces at Bay

Weapons and warfare played an integral role in the history and culture of ancient Egypt. Indeed, the Egyptian realm—the world's first true nation-state—was literally forged on the anvil of war. During the fourth millennium B.C., two distinct Egyptian kingdoms evolved along the Nile River, one in the south (called Upper Egypt because it lay closer to the Nile's source), the other in the north (Lower Egypt). These states came together into a single country by force, specifically through the military efforts of a ruler of the southern kingdom. About 3100 B.C. Menes (sometimes called Narmer) conquered the north and made himself Egypt's first pharaoh. (The term "pharaoh" is an ancient Greek version of the even more ancient Egyptian *per-aa,* meaning "great house." It originally referred to the royal palace and was not used by the Egyptians themselves to describe their kings until the era of the New Kingdom, which began around 1550 B.C.)

To emphasize the importance of unity, Menes established a new city, Memphis, at the boundary between the former rival kingdoms, making it his capital; he also adopted a crown that combined the main features of the crowns worn by the leaders of those kingdoms. And, significantly, he established the mace, a club used to smash heads in battle, as the symbol of the pharaoh's authority. Even after the mace became obsolete in warfare many centuries later, its image remained in official and artistic representations, a potent reminder that the Egyptian king was ever ready to bludgeon his enemies into submission.

Maintaining the Natural Cosmic Order

Surprisingly, considering this threatening, warlike image projected by the early pharaohs, these rulers and their people did not conceive of themselves as waging war in the modern sense of the word. In fact, as pointed out by Middle Eastern scholar Sheikh 'Ibada al-Nubi, "Despite an infinite number of ways to define the 'enemy' and a multitude of terms for battle and fighting, the Egyptian language did not possess a single precise term to define that particular legal, political, social, and economic situation known as 'war.'"[1]

This odd state of affairs grew in large degree out of Egypt's unique geographical situation. Its population was concentrated in the narrow, fertile ribbon of land running along the Nile's banks and for a long time remained more or less insulated and isolated from the outside world by vast expanses of arid desert. Among other things, this fostered a rather distorted sense of self-importance. From the beginning of the era ushered in by Menes, the Early Dynastic Period (ca. 3100–ca. 2686 B.C.) and likely dating well back into the Predynastic Period (ca. 5500–ca. 3100 B.C.), the Egyptians perceived themselves as occupying the center of creation. All had been chaos, they believed, until their god Amun had sprung into existence and created the world's first inhabitable land in their midst. Thus, the natural cosmic order revolved around them and their culture. And outsiders—those who lived on the "fringes" beyond Egypt's borders—were hostile, backward, evil, cowardly, and/or a perpetual threat to the cosmic order. This air of superiority is evident in a twenty-second-century B.C. kernel of advice from an Egyptian ruler to his son:

> [Behold] the miserable Asiatic; he is wretched because of the [inferior] place he is [inhabiting]. Short of water, bare of wood, its paths are many and painful because of mountains. He does not dwell in one place, [but instead] food propels his legs [i.e., he lives a nomadic existence, seen as inferior to the settled agricultural life along the Nile].[2]

In this peculiar worldview, any military operation an Egyptian pharaoh deemed necessary was a sort of police action—a punishment of local rebels or an extermination of foreign pests buzzing around the borders—in either case the primary aim being to restore the natural order of things. It

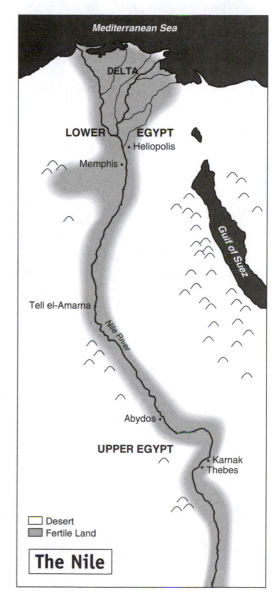

was not a full-fledged war, since that could be waged only against an opponent as strong and worthy as Egypt; and to the early Egyptians, this was an alien concept.

National Survival in a Hostile World

As a result, for a long time Egyptian rulers did not seriously consider the idea of conquering peoples and lands located beyond Egypt's immediate vicinity. Some pharaohs of the eras that modern scholars call the Old Kingdom (ca. 2686–ca. 2181 B.C.) and Middle Kingdom (ca. 2055–ca. 1650 B.C.) did send troops into Nubia (the region lying directly south of Egypt) and other nearby ar-

eas. But these expeditions were not part of an effort to create an empire. Rather, they were usually intended as punitive measures against rebels or as justifiable means of restoring order and safety to the country's border regions. To the Egyptians, the very integrity of their nation depended on the safety of the borders because these barriers were all that separated their civilized bastion from the dark, chaotic forces perceived as lurking outside.

With the advent of the New Kingdom (ca. 1550–ca. 1069 B.C.), in response to large-scale attacks by foreign peoples, Egypt finally expanded its interests beyond its borders and acquired an empire. Yet the

An elegant relief dating from the New Kingdom shows a religious procession in which Egyptian soldiers march carrying axes and throwing sticks.

How Do Historians Know?

...om volume 1 of his Ancient ...the late, great Egyptologist ...marizes some of the major ...ern historians consult for in-...political, military, and cultural ...ypt's Old Kingdom.

...ssess any documents at all from ...ingdom is chiefly due to the mas-...ry tombs of that age, in which ...recorded. The exceptions are in-...on foreign soil and a few scanty ...s of papyrus containing accounts ...ers. . . . The chief inscriptions . . . con-...most exclusively of the name and many ...of the owner of the tomb. Now and ...the legal enactment by which the tomb

was endowed and maintained is recorded on the wall. Such wills and conveyances are, of course, invaluable cultural documents. Gradually the nobles were inclined to add a few biographical details to the series of bare titles. . . . In the Sixth Dynasty [ca. 2345–ca. 2181 B.C.] these biographies became real narratives of the career of the departed noble, or at least of his most notable achievements in the service of the Pharaoh. . . . As the aggressiveness of the pharaohs increased, their foreign enterprises found record on the rocks in a number of distant regions . . . where they still exist. [Many royal inscriptions and paintings also adorned temple walls, but almost all examples from the Old Kingdom have] totally perished.

...ty work." On the one hand, military serv-... was not a full-time profession. Those few ...ative Egyptians who joined the army did so ...only when drafted into service by the government; they underwent some brief training, marched and fought as ordered, then disbanded and returned to their homes. More importantly, the vast majority of soldiers were mercenaries—foreign troops, mostly from areas near Egypt's borders, who were either hired or forced into service. It is even possible, though not yet proven, that most native Egyptians were exempted from military service in this era.

Taking their places in the army ranks were mainly Nubians, black Africans inhabiting Nubia, the land lying along Egypt's southern border. (The native Egyptians were themselves brown- or olive-skinned Semites, like today's Arabs and Jews.) In a surviving doc-

ument, a high official of the court of an Old Kingdom pharaoh, Pepi I, tells about his role in an expedition against some marauding nomads, the "Sand-Dwellers." The Egyptian army, he says, was largely made up of Nubians, for whom "I was the one who made the [military] plan." Later, the official claims:

His Majesty sent me to lead this army five times, in order to repel . . . the Sand-Dwellers, each time they rebelled. . . . I crossed over [the desert?] . . . with these troops. I made a landing at the rear of the heights of the mountain range. . . . I caught them all and every backslider [rebel] among them was slain. [6]

Nubia was a prime source not only of soldiers for the early Egyptian army, but

pharaohs did not impose direct rule on or send legions of settlers into the conquered territories in an effort to make them part of Egypt proper. Instead, they exercised influence over these areas through treaties and alliances with local rulers and vigorous trade relations. The main object of battles and conquest remained, as always, security—to keep enemies from threatening the traditional Egyptian heartland. Such enemies were, as al-Nubi puts it, "a disturbing element in the stable progress of the Egyptian world, and the king, as representative and official personification of that world, was obliged to keep them in check."[3] Inscriptions commissioned by one New Kingdom pharaoh boast:

His majesty has gone forth like a whirlwind against them [his enemies], fighting on the battlefield like a runner. The dread of him and the terror of him have entered into their bodies. They are capsized and overwhelmed where they are. Their heart is taken away, their soul is flown away. Their weapons are scattered upon the sea. . . . His majesty is like an enraged lion, attacking his assailant with his arms, plundering on his right hand and powerful on his left hand.[4]

This and other similar tracts by Egyptian rulers were intended as propaganda, of course, and as such were often highly exaggerated. Yet they reflect an underlying truth, namely, that during the roughly five-hundred-year span of the New Kingdom, the Egyptian army was one of the most formidable in the world. To be sure, the Egyptians were not

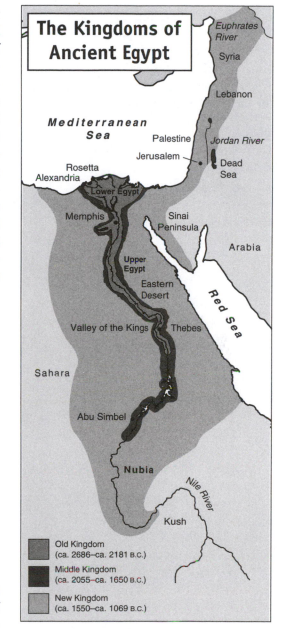

The Kingdoms of Ancient Egypt

Euphrates River
Syria
Lebanon
Mediterranean Sea
Palestine
Jordan River
Jerusalem
Dead Sea
Rosetta
Alexandria
Lower Egypt
Memphis
Sinai Peninsula
Arabia
Upper Egypt
Eastern Desert
Red Sea
Valley of the Kings
Thebes
Sahara
Abu Simbel
Nubia
Nile River
Kush

Old Kingdom (ca. 2686–ca. 2181 B.C.)
Middle Kingdom (ca. 2055–ca. 1650 B.C.)
New Kingdom (ca. 1550–ca. 1069 B.C.)

great military innovators; they borrowed their most effective weapons, including the chariot and the special battlefield tactics associated with it, from their enemies. What Egypt lacked in creativity, however, it amply made up for in the large size and efficient organization of its manpower. In spite of lacking a word for war, therefore, the Egyptians waged it with great skill and success. And the quality of their military was a major factor in their extraordinarily long survival in a hostile world. By the time the first of a long series of foreign armies managed to overwhelm Egypt in the first millennium B.C., it had lasted as an independent nation more than ten times longer than the United States has.

CHAPTER ONE

Early Eg
Weapons and

In this excerpt f
Records of Egypt
J.H. Breasted s
sources that
formation o
affairs du

Preparedness for war, including the large-scale manufacture of weapons and the drafting and training of troops, was an ever-present reality in Egypt even in the earliest historical eras. Yet in the Early Dynastic Period, Old Kingdom, and Middle Kingdom, together comprising the first 1,450 years of the nation's existence, warfare was not the top priority of the Egyptian government. Major military expeditions were not launched very often. And when they were, they had two basic aims: The first was to guard and maintain the country's borders against possible threats; the second was to exploit natural resources, including building materials and local manpower, on or slightly beyond those borders.

The main reason for the relatively minor role of warfare, especially in the centuries before the Middle Kingdom (which began near the end of the third millennium B.C.), was Egypt's peculiar geographic situation. For a long time, the country remained largely isolated from the outside world. And its territorial integrity was not seriously threatened.

As a result,
in sculptures, pa
royal and upper-cla
These records instea
important aspects of
life," scholar Andrea M
"such as social and mo
exploration and exploit
sources and trade conta
of monumental tombs
great pyramids at Gi
reers."[5] Only later, in th
and to an even greater d
followed it, would milit
battles become the glo
kingly art and propaga

Exploiting the
Nubians

In fact, military affairs
perceived as anything
Old Kingdom. Some e
both aristocratic indi
manded the national a
ordinary Egyptians lo

Early Egyptian Weapons and Warfare

Preparedness for war, including the large-scale manufacture of weapons and the drafting and training of troops, was an ever-present reality in Egypt even in the earliest historical eras. Yet in the Early Dynastic Period, Old Kingdom, and Middle Kingdom, together comprising the first 1,450 years of the nation's existence, warfare was not the top priority of the Egyptian government. Major military expeditions were not launched very often. And when they were, they had two basic aims: The first was to guard and maintain the country's borders against possible threats; the second was to exploit natural resources, including building materials and local manpower, on or slightly beyond those borders.

The main reason for the relatively minor role of warfare, especially in the centuries before the Middle Kingdom (which began near the end of the third millennium B.C.), was Egypt's peculiar geographic situation. For a long time, the country remained largely isolated from the outside world. And its territorial integrity was not seriously threatened.

As a result, war was not a major theme in sculptures, paintings, and inscriptions in royal and upper-class tombs and elsewhere. These records instead emphasized "other important aspects of political and social life," scholar Andrea M. Gnirs points out, "such as social and moral obligations, the exploration and exploitation of natural resources and trade contacts, the construction of monumental tombs [among them the great pyramids at Giza], or official careers."[5] Only later, in the Middle Kingdom and to an even greater degree in the age that followed it, would military expeditions and battles become the glorious centerpiece of kingly art and propaganda in Egypt.

Exploiting the "Wretched" Nubians

In fact, military affairs seem to have been perceived as anything *but* glorious in the Old Kingdom. Some evidence suggests that both aristocratic individuals, who commanded the national armies in battle, and ordinary Egyptians looked on soldiering as

HOW DO HISTORIANS KNOW?

In this excerpt from volume 1 of his Ancient Records of Egypt, *the late, great Egyptologist J.H. Breasted summarizes some of the major sources that modern historians consult for information about political, military, and cultural affairs during Egypt's Old Kingdom.*

That we possess any documents at all from the Old Kingdom is chiefly due to the massive masonry tombs of that age, in which they were recorded. The exceptions are inscriptions on foreign soil and a few scanty fragments of papyrus containing accounts and letters. . . . The chief inscriptions . . . consist almost exclusively of the name and many titles of the owner of the tomb. Now and again the legal enactment by which the tomb was endowed and maintained is recorded on the wall. Such wills and conveyances are, of course, invaluable cultural documents. Gradually the nobles were inclined to add a few biographical details to the series of bare titles. . . . In the Sixth Dynasty [ca. 2345–ca. 2181 B.C.] these biographies became real narratives of the career of the departed noble, or at least of his most notable achievements in the service of the Pharaoh. . . . As the aggressiveness of the pharaohs increased, their foreign enterprises found record on the rocks in a number of distant regions . . . where they still exist. [Many royal inscriptions and paintings also adorned temple walls, but almost all examples from the Old Kingdom have] totally perished.

"dirty work." On the one hand, military service was not a full-time profession. Those few native Egyptians who joined the army did so only when drafted into service by the government; they underwent some brief training, marched and fought as ordered, then disbanded and returned to their homes. More importantly, the vast majority of soldiers were mercenaries—foreign troops, mostly from areas near Egypt's borders, who were either hired or forced into service. It is even possible, though not yet proven, that most native Egyptians were exempted from military service in this era.

Taking their places in the army ranks were mainly Nubians, black Africans inhabiting Nubia, the land lying along Egypt's southern border. (The native Egyptians were themselves brown- or olive-skinned Semites, like today's Arabs and Jews.) In a surviving document, a high official of the court of an Old Kingdom pharaoh, Pepi I, tells about his role in an expedition against some marauding nomads, the "Sand-Dwellers." The Egyptian army, he says, was largely made up of Nubians, for whom "I was the one who made the [military] plan." Later, the official claims:

His Majesty sent me to lead this army five times, in order to repel . . . the Sand-Dwellers, each time they rebelled. . . . I crossed over [the desert?] . . . with these troops. I made a landing at the rear of the heights of the mountain range. . . . I caught them all and every backslider [rebel] among them was slain. [6]

Nubia was a prime source not only of soldiers for the early Egyptian army, but

also of valuable material products such as herds of cattle, ivory, and ostrich feathers. Thus, many military expeditions were launched into the area during the Early Dynastic Period, Old Kingdom, and Middle Kingdom. Numerous inscriptions describe the Nubians as vile, wretched, and easily defeated. In fact, the image of the Nubian eventually became the chief symbol of a defeated enemy in Egyptian art and royal propaganda. Other foreigners held in general contempt by the Egyptians and often conscripted into the Egyptian military were the Libyans, who inhabited the parched desert lands lying along Egypt's western border.

Smashing and Chopping Weapons

Whether they were native Egyptians, Nubians, or Libyans, the soldiers of early Egyptian armies used the same weapons. From an uncertain date far back in the Predynastic Period and on through the Early Dynastic, Old Kingdom, and Middle Kingdom eras, the primary weapons remained few and almost unchanged. The mace (club), ax, spear, and bow and arrow were the main types.

Swords were sometimes used, but those of the fourth and third millennia B.C. had a serious limitation. "[They] could be fashioned only after [the attainment of] a mastery

These miniature soldiers represent Nubians, black Africans whom the Egyptians often pressed into military service, especially in the Old and Middle Kingdoms.

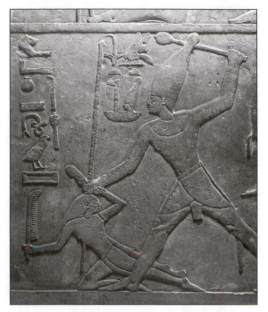

The image of the Egyptian pharaoh striking the "wretched" Nubian with a mace was common in Egyptian art.

of the art of producing hard metals," explains former Hebrew University scholar Yigael Yadin. "A long and tough blade which would not break or bend on impact could be made from hard metal alone."[7] The problem was that copper, the only metal used widely for weapons in Egypt in this period, was relatively soft; so a long blade swung in a slashing or hacking motion could easily break. As a result, swords were usually short and straight, like daggers, and used mainly for stabbing if and when a soldier got close enough to an opponent. The sword was therefore a secondary backup weapon employed only occasionally on the battlefield.

Of the primary weapons, the earliest known was the mace, which became the symbol of the king's authority. The first versions had a head made out of heavy stone, often hematite, a blood-colored rock containing iron oxide. Gradually, copper mace-heads began to supplant the stone ones. Their heads were most often either pear shaped or round, and the handle had a concave (inwardly curved or tapered) gripping area to help prevent the weapon from flying out of the user's hand when he swung it. Clearly, the mace was an effective tool for crushing enemy skulls, hands, legs, and even spears and swords if swung with sufficient force.

For cutting and chopping, on the other hand, the battle-ax was more effective. According to Ian Shaw, a noted archaeologist and expert on Egyptian warfare:

> In the Old and Middle Kingdoms the conventional ax usually consisted of a semicircular copper head tied to a wooden handle by cords, threaded through perforations [small holes] in the copper and wrapped around lugs [pegs]. At this stage there was little difference between the battleax and the woodworker's ax. In the Middle Kingdom, however, some battleaxes had longer blades with concave sides narrowing down to a curved edge.[8]

Such cutting axes were used in various ways. A relief sculpture from the tomb of an official of the Old Kingdom at Deshasheh, in Upper Egypt, shows soldiers using axes in battle. The ax heads are long and shallow, and the men swing the weapons with two hands. By contrast, a tomb painting dating from a century or so later shows soldiers wielding axes with shorter, deeper blades; these weapons are being swung with one hand in an effort to chop down the wooden gate of an enemy fortress.

Shields, Spears, and Bows

These early axes were not intended for piercing armor, since the Egyptians did not employ body armor during the fourth and third millennia B.C. Stone reliefs and tomb paintings of the Old and Middle Kingdoms typically show soldiers wearing only belts and small triangular loincloths or slightly longer linen kilts. Their only effective protection, therefore, was the shield. The most common type was a rectangular wooden frame covered by layers of dried cowhide. Often such shields tapered to a curved or pointed edge at the top. In the middle of the back of the framework was a wooden handle to hold the shield, although leather straps were sometimes attached to allow the soldier to carry it on his shoulder, leaving both hands free. The latter situation was preferable when on the march or when climbing a scaling ladder during a siege.

The shield provided a measure of protection not only against close-up attacks by maces, axes, and swords, but also from barrages of missile weapons either thrown or shot from a distance. First among these was a type of javelin (throwing spear) that was in common use throughout the Near East by the end of the fourth millennium B.C. The so-called Hunters' Slate Palette, dating from this period in Egypt, shows the weapon in use against animals. It consisted of a long

MESOPOTAMIA'S INFLUENCE ON EGYPT

In the era of the Old Kingdom, when Egypt rarely engaged in wars and its soldiers were largely unseasoned nonprofessionals, far away on the plains of Mesopotamia (what is now Iraq) several aggressive city-states had already developed more advanced military methods. These eventually influenced the Egyptians, who centuries later adopted some of them. Here, from an article in John Hackett's Warfare in the Ancient World, *Dr. Trevor Watkins describes a Mesopotamian battle formation of the mid–third millennium B.C. carved on a marker stone.*

The battle-scene shows the army at the moment of victory, marching over the bodies of their defeated and slain enemies. In the upper register [band of carved figures] a troop of heavy infantry is led by the king himself; in the lower register the king is shown riding in his battle-wagon [a clumsy, solid-wheeled cart pulled by four donkeys; a precursor of the war chariot] in the van [forefront] of a troop of light infantry. The light infantry wear no protective armor and carry no shields; each holds a long spear in the left hand and a battle-ax in the right. The heavy infantry is depicted . . . [as] massed ranks of helmeted spearmen behind a front rank of men bearing shields. . . . What is significant is the number of spears projecting between the shields. The artist emphasizes the solidity of the formation, protected from chin to ankle by almost interlocking shields. The implied battle tactics anticipate those of the [Greek] Macedonian phalanx and the Roman legion. . . . It also suggests that the armies of those [Mesopotamian] city-states contained a hard core of trained professional soldiery. No seasonal levy of [local farmers] could have managed such precision and solidarity and these soldiers were trained, uniformed and equipped to fight as a corps.

wooden staff topped by a leaf-shaped blade of flint or copper secured to the shaft by cords tied around a long tang (narrow projection) protruding from the blade's bottom. In battle an attacking soldier likely threw his javelin at the enemy formation at a distance of about fifty to a hundred feet; then he must have removed a mace or battle-ax from his belt, closed the remaining gap between the opposing lines, and engaged in hand-to-hand fighting.

Arrows could be shot a great deal farther than javelins could be thrown, of course, and were effective for softening up an enemy formation before the troops made physical contact with it. The bow, another weapon shown in the Hunters' Slate Palette, was a common weapon used by Egyptian hunters and soldiers in the Predynastic Period and remained important in warfare in later eras. Early "horn" bows were so named because they consisted of a pair of antelope horns connected to either end of a central shaft made of strong but pliable wood. By the Early Dynastic period, the stronger and more flexible "self" or "simple" bow was in wide use. Usually between three-and-a-half and seven feet long, it was made of a wooden shaft that tapered toward the ends and was strung with a cord made of tightly twisted animal gut. Some of the longer bows were "recurved," meaning that their shafts curved inward, then outward, and then inward again; these weapons, which employed tight cord bindings to reinforce the shaft at various points, had greater power and range than shorter, single-curved versions.

Little Evidence for Military Organization

Surviving remnants of bows, spears, maces, and so forth, along with depictions of them in carvings, sculptures, and wall paintings, provide a fairly clear picture of the weapons that the early Egyptians used. Unfortunately, however, this evidence reveals little or nothing about the command structure and organization of the early Egyptian army, either on or off the battlefield. But certain general conclusions can be inferred from the existing evidence. First, if soldiering was a secondary and unglamorous endeavor, as it appears to have been, few highborn, ambitious, and talented Egyptians would want to become officers. And those that did serve as commanders

These realistic, miniature Egyptian soldiers carrying spears and shields were found in a tomb dating to the Middle Kingdom.

Egyptian soldiers of the Middle Kingdom period wore loincloths rather than armor.

probably did so on a temporary basis rather than pursuing military careers. Moreover, the ordinary soldiers were also nonprofessionals who served short hitches; so there would have been little time for extensive training or effective organization into many and complex specialized units.

It is likely, therefore, that the early Egyptian army was organized along relatively simple lines, with a few commanders leading large troop contingents of no fixed size. According to Shaw:

There does not appear to have been any overall military hierarchy [ladder of positions of authority] or organiza-

tion in the Old Kingdom, although the title "overseer of soldiers" was occasionally used, and the fortresses on Egypt's borders were controlled by the "overseer of desert blockhouses and royal fortresses." *Tst* (a term roughly corresponding to "battalion") was the only word used to describe units of soldiers in the Old Kingdom. [9]

The importance of soldiering and military affairs increased to some degree during the First Intermediate Period (ca. 2181–ca. 2055 B.C.). During the short interlude between the Old and Middle Kingdoms, the royal authority in Memphis declined and the

SINGLE COMBAT IN THE MIDDLE KINGDOM

During the First Intermediate Period and Middle Kingdom, a number of standard pitched battles apparently took place. But soldiers also fought in one-on-one duels reminiscent of the single combats between Greek and Trojan warriors in Homer's epic poem the Iliad. *This excerpt from the famous story of the Egyptian courtier Sinuhe (quoted in James Pritchard's* Ancient Near Eastern Texts*), dating from the dawn of the Middle Kingdom, describes such a duel.*

A mighty man of Retenu [Syria] came, that he might challenge me in my own camp. He was a hero without peer, and he had [beaten all opponents in his land]. He said that he would fight me, he intended to despoil me, and he planned to plunder my cattle. . . . During the night I strung my bow and shot my arrows [in a practice session] . . . and I polished my weapons. When day broke, [the men of] Retenu came [to watch the fight]. . . . Then he came to me as I was waiting. . . . Every heart burned for me; women and men groaned. . . . Then he took his shield and his battleax and his armful of javelins. Now after I had let his weapons issue forth [without doing me any damage] . . . he charged me and I shot him, my arrow sticking in his neck. He cried out and fell on his nose. I [finished him off] with his own battleax and raised my cry of victory . . . while every Asiatic roared. . . . Then I carried off his goods and plundered his cattle. What he had planned to do to me, I did to him.

country became unstable and disunited. For a little more than a century, powerful local warlords fought one another, as well as the pharaoh, who still retained some allegiance in the north.

During these civil wars, the armies of the warlords were probably not significantly more organized than the state-controlled army of the Old Kingdom. However, the new climate of violence did cause some institutional changes. First, evidence shows that more native Egyptians were under arms than in prior centuries; Nubians were still a dominating presence in the military ranks and, in Sheikh 'Ibada al-Nubi's words, "a genuine ethnic nucleus . . . operating in and on the behalf of Egypt, but without losing their character." [10] Out of necessity, to protect the territories of their masters (whether warlords or the pharaoh), Egyptians and

Nubians alike often served under arms for extended periods. Furthermore, soldiers and their exploits began to be praised in various writings. Clearly, the elements necessary for a full-time professional army were beginning to take shape, although that turn of events was still a few centuries away.

Military Developments in the Middle Kingdom

Another change in military affairs during the First Intermediate Period was the manner in which individual leaders—in this case the warlords—portrayed (or allowed subordinates to portray) their battlefield exploits. They proudly celebrated their victories in inscriptions, each trying to outdo the others. The pharaohs subsequently carried on this practice when they regained control of the country at the beginning of the Middle Kingdom, each king attempting to project the public image of an invincible hero. Describing the second Middle Kingdom pharaoh—Senusret (or Sesotris) I—an official named Sinuhe wrote:

> He is a god indeed, without peer. He is a champion who acts with his own arms, a fighter without anyone like him [i.e., like no one else] when he is seen attacking the bowmen. . . . He is one who . . . renders hands powerless, so that his enemies cannot muster their ranks. He is vengeful when he cracks skulls, and no one stands up near him. He steps wide when he annihilates the fugitive. . . . He is stalwart of heart . . . and does not allow cowardice around him. . . . He need not repeat the act of killing [i.e., strike a second blow], for there is no one who can deflect his arrow nor one who can draw his bow. The bowmen retreat before him as if before the might of a great goddess.[11]

In addition to the pharaoh's enhanced image as a military leader, the military establishment as a whole took on increased importance in the Middle Kingdom. For one thing, the army, when called into service, was bigger than it had been in the past; clearly, maintaining the allegiance of more men, both native Egyptians and Nubians, was a logical way to overshadow and discourage any local princes or warlords who might consider challenging the central authority. The government also increased the number of forts along the borders, still seen as all-important barriers against the forces of chaos and barbarism beyond. Moreover,

depictions of soldiers fighting battles became more common in artwork commissioned by the pharaohs.

The weapons wielded by these soldiers in the Middle Kingdom were largely the same as those of the Early Dynastic Period and Old Kingdom. The most common and effective long-range weapon was still the simple bow. (The more advanced and deadly composite bow was already in use in Mesopotamia, what is now Iraq, at this time; but it was difficult and expensive to make and did not gain widespread use in Egypt until after the Middle Kingdom.) A short sword with a curved, sicklelike blade appeared in Egypt in the late third millennium B.C. It was designed for

A sculpted likeness of the Middle Kingdom pharaoh Senusret I, whom Sinhue described.

slashing rather than stabbing; but its small, easily breakable blade made it, like the straight stabbing swords still in use, a secondary weapon. The only significant development in weaponry in the Middle Kingdom was a new battle-ax—the "epsilon ax," introduced into Egypt from Palestine and Syria. It had a short blade with three tangs in the back; the tangs had holes through which cords passed to fasten the ax head to the long handle.

Thanks to increased depictions of warfare in written records and art in the Middle Kingdom, the military units and formations of the soldiers who wielded these weapons are somewhat clearer than those in prior ages. Middle Kingdom armies, says Yadin,

were already organized in units which marched in disciplined order. The written records also contain much detail on the size of armies and the units taking part in battle, which indicate that there was open combat on a large scale. Thus we find several references in . . . documents from the 18th century [B.C.] to militia units of 10,000 warriors. Mostly, of course, the units referred to are smaller, containing 3,000, 2,000, 1,000, 600, and 100 men. Also mentioned is the 300-man unit, used mainly as an assault unit, comprising three companies of 100 men each. It appears from the documents that the basic unit, the

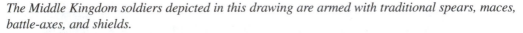

The Middle Kingdom soldiers depicted in this drawing are armed with traditional spears, maces, battle-axes, and shields.

section [perhaps equivalent to a modern army platoon], was probably composed of ten men. [12]

Nightmare Becomes Reality

The soldiers in these units were still largely Nubians, Libyans, and other foreigners who either hailed from border areas or had been allowed to settle inside Egypt proper. One of these groups was composed of "Asiatics," that is, people from Palestine and other lands lying northeast of Egypt. They settled in the region of the eastern Nile Delta in the last two centuries of the Middle Kingdom and were destined to play a pivotal role in the country's political and military affairs.

As ethnic fighters recruited into the Egyptian army, these Asiatic immigrants must have gained considerable numbers and military strength over time. The proof is that in about 1650 B.C. they rose up and took over the northern section of Egypt by force (while the pharaohs maintained a power base in the south, with their capital at Thebes). This marked the end of the Middle Kingdom and beginning of the Second Intermediate Period (ca. 1650–ca. 1550 B.C.). Modern scholars refer to these interlopers by the name later given to them by Greek writers, the Hyksos, or "shepherd kings," although the ancient Egyptian name for them meant "rulers of foreign lands."

The Egyptians' worst nightmare—the attack of "barbarians" from beyond the borders—had become a terrifying and humiliating reality. Eventually, the natives would rally and take back their lost lands, but in the process they would become even more warlike than the Hyksos. Egypt's great age of empire and military glory was about to begin.

CHAPTER TWO

The New Kingdom and Chariot Warfare

The Egyptians managed to drive the hated Hyksos out of Egypt by the mid–sixteenth century B.C. But the humiliating century-long occupation of the country had left its people

Ahmose, first pharaoh of the New Kingdom, liberated Egypt from the Hyksos.

scarred and their outlook on life and the world forever changed. First, there was a major upsurge in nationalism and patriotism during and immediately following the expulsion of the Hyksos. Kamose, last pharaoh of the Seventeenth Dynasty, and Ahmose (or Amosis), first ruler of the Eighteenth—which initiated the New Kingdom—waged numerous campaigns as part of a war of national liberation; they and their followers directed their wrath not only against the Hyksos, but also against those Egyptians who had collaborated with the occupiers. Thus, by eliminating competing local factions, the conflict had a strong unifying effect on the nation and its inhabitants.

There was also a new and disturbing perception that the country's borders were not and may never be totally secure. So the Egyptians had to do more than simply guard the borders; they must go past these artificial barriers and confront any enemies that posed a potential threat, thereby expanding Egypt's sphere of influence into neighboring lands. As a result, Egypt became a major military state, and imperialism, one nation's attempted military and/or political domination of others, became a defining feature of the government of the New Kingdom. Another defining feature was a new kind of warfare employed by Egypt's rulers, one largely built around the battle chariot, ironically a weapon introduced to them by their enemy, the Hyksos. Led by a series of aggressive warrior kings, an invigorated and powerful new army made Egypt both respected and feared across large portions of the Near East.

Expanding Egypt's Sphere of Influence

This new spirit and policy of military aggression began with Ahmose, who liberated the country. After driving north from Thebes, the pharaoh besieged the main Hyksos stronghold of Avaris, in the eastern section of the Nile Delta. A brief record of this campaign has survived in the tomb biography of the captain of a Nile vessel. His name, like that of his king, was Ahmose. "[We] besieged the city of Avaris," the lesser Ahmose bragged.

I showed valor on foot before his majesty; then I was appointed [to be captain of the ship] *Shining-in-Memphis.* . . . [I] fought on the water in the canal: Pezedku of Avaris. Then I fought hand to hand, [and] I brought away a hand. [Egyptian soldiers often cut off the hands of slain enemies as battle trophies.] It was reported to the royal herald. [The commander] gave to me the Gold of Valor [a medal for bravery]. . . . Then

HYKSOS' CONTRIBUTIONS TO EGYPT

In this excerpt from his acclaimed History of Ancient Egypt, *scholar Nicolas Grimal identifies the Hyksos and comments on their significant military contributions to the Egyptians.*

Who were the Hyksos? Their name is the debased Greek version of the Egyptian term: *hekaw-khasut* ("the chiefs of foreign lands"). This name gives no indication of race or any clearly defined homeland. It was a term applied to all foreigners in Nubia and Syria-Palestine during the Old and Middle Kingdoms. The Hyksos seem to have approximated the "Asiatic" peoples [i.e., some of the local peoples of Syria-Palestine] whom the Egyptians had previously fought. . . . The Hyksos presence in Egypt was evidently less damaging than later Egyptian sources tend to suggest. It must, however, have made its mark on Egyptian civilization, which from then on was far less insular. . . . The Hyksos rulers created a legacy from which the New Kingdom pharaohs would eventually draw inspiration. The technological innovations of the Hyksos period were innumerable, particularly in the field of warfare, which was revolutionized by the introduction of the harnessed horse [especially as used to draw the chariot]. . . . The Egyptians were also introduced to innovative items of armor created with new techniques of bronze-working, which would eventually allow the New Kingdom pharaohs to expand eastwards.

there was again fighting in this place; I again fought hand to hand there; I brought away [another] hand. [And I received] the Gold of Valor in the second place. . . . [We] captured Avaris; I took captive there one man and three women, a total of four heads [persons]; his majesty gave them to me for slaves.[13]

After taking Avaris, the pharaoh Ahmose drove the Hyksos out of Egypt. He was doubtful that this would ensure the country's safety, since the enemy might well try to regroup and launch a counteroffensive. So he pursued them across the Sinai Peninsula and into Palestine. There, he trapped most of the remaining Hyksos in a town called Sharuhen and laid siege to it for three

Egyptians of the New Kingdom continued to exploit Nubians, depicted in this relief.

years. Emerging victorious, Ahmose returned to Egypt, launched a successful attack on its old whipping horse, Nubia, and finished reuniting the nation. "It was in recognition of his achievement in reuniting [Egypt]," says scholar Mark Healy,

that Ahmose was honored by later generations in having established the 18th Dynasty. By his ejection of the Hyksos from Egypt he had elevated the kingdom to become the greatest in the Near East. Inheriting the mantle of the Hyksos, Ahmose was acknowledged as overlord by the states of Palestine and Syria, no doubt encouraged in their declarations by a military demonstration later in his reign that took him as far north as Djahy [Phoenicia, on the coast of what is now Israel]. It is very likely that there was a tacit acceptance that all Asia as far as the Euphrates [River] now rightly constituted Egypt's sphere of influence. The projection of military power far beyond Egypt's eastern frontier as the best and most effective method for her defense now became a keystone of her policy in dealing with the [region of Syria-Palestine].[14]

Indeed, Ahmose set a precedent, and after his reign each new pharaoh was ready and eager to prove himself in war. This not only made the country safer, but also greatly enhanced the king's official image as portrayed in royal decrees, building inscriptions, paintings, and other modes of propaganda. In Egypt's earliest years, the pharaoh had been viewed literally as a god in earthly form. But by the advent of the New Kingdom, most saw him as a mere man, very powerful and perhaps divinely inspired, but mortal nonetheless. Waging and winning wars was a way of elevating the pharaoh's image; as an invincible war hero and national savior, he could be confident of maintaining the allegiance of his people.

Each new pharaoh therefore strove to lead one or more military expeditions into Syria-Palestine, Nubia, or both. For example, an inscription found at Tombos (near the Nile's Third Cataract) describes a Nubian campaign by Thutmose I (or Thutmosis I, reigned 1504–1492 B.C.):

> He has overthrown the chief of the Nubians; the black man is helpless, defenseless in his grasp. . . . The Nubian troglodytes [primitive cave dwellers, a standard insult rather than literal description] fall by the sword, and are thrust aside in their lands; their foulness . . . floods their valleys.[15]

Later the same ruler invaded Syria-Palestine, as told by one of his officers:

> His majesty made a great slaughter among them. Numberless were the living prisoners, which his majesty brought off from his victories. Meanwhile I was at the head of our troops, and his majesty beheld my bravery. I brought off [captured] a chariot, its horses, and him who was upon it as a living prisoner, and took them to his majesty. [As a reward I received] gold in double measure.[16]

Pharaoh Thutmose I, seen here, invaded both Nubia and Syria-Palestine.

A New Weapon and Status Symbol—the Chariot

Perhaps the most significant reference in the preceding account is that to the capture of a chariot on the battlefield. The fact is that the Egyptians could not have ejected the Hyksos and successfully invaded Syria-Palestine without this formidable new weapon. The chariot had been used in battle in Mesopotamia for more than a thousand years before its introduction into Egypt. Chariot technology eventually made its way into Syria-Palestine, where the Hyksos acquired it. They then brought it into northern Egypt, and eventually the pharaohs at Thebes adopted it out of necessity. Used in conjunction with another advanced weapon, the composite bow, as well as traditional military elements, the chariot became a devastating

A SOLDIER IN THE PHARAOH'S SERVICE

Much of the sparse contemporary information that has survived about Egypt's war to expel the Hyksos comes from the tomb biography of a naval officer named Ahmose, the namesake of the pharaoh who led the campaign against the intruders. Here, from John A. Wilson's translation (in James Pritchard's Ancient Near Eastern Texts), *Ahmose describes his own background, giving a recognizable human face to a soldier in a now distant and largely forgotten conflict.*

I had my upbringing in the town of el-Kab [in Upper Egypt], my father being a soldier . . . his name being Bebe, the son of the woman Roonet. Then I served as [a] soldier in his place in the ship *The Wild Bull* in the time of the Lord of the Two lands [i.e., Ahmose I] . . . when I was still a boy, before I had taken a wife. . . . But after I had set up a household, then I was taken on the ship *Northern,* because I was valiant. Thus I used to accompany the Pharaoh . . . on foot, following his excursions in his chariot.

tool of warfare and national policy in the hands of major kingdoms like Egypt. (Chariots were very expensive to produce and maintain, so only large, wealthy states could afford chariot corps with thousands of vehicles.)

Not surprisingly, the first Egyptian chariots were virtually identical to those used in Syria-Palestine. They were very lightweight yet sturdy. Describing a surviving example from the era of Thutmose I and his immediate successors, Yigael Yadin writes:

This chariot has three main elements: the body, the wheels, and the pole and yoke. The body has a wooden frame. . . . Its base is one meter [3.3 feet] wide and half a meter deep. It is 75 centimeters [29 inches] high in the front—which would cover about half way up to the thighs of the charioteer. . . . The whole of the front and the bottom part of the sides of the body were [covered by leather]. The axel-rod is 6 centimeters [2.4 inches] thick at the center

and its length between the wheels is 1.23 meters [4.1 feet]. . . . The wheels had four spokes. . . . The chariot pole is 2.5 meters [8.2 feet] long, its hind end attached to the rear bar of the body frame and running under the body, giving additional strength to an otherwise frail structure. . . . The yoke is shaped like a double-convex bow and is attached to the forward end of the pole by nails. . . . Everything was planned to make the vehicle light, flexible, and strong.[17]

In the century that followed, Egyptian chariots underwent a few modifications. To accommodate more weapons and equipment, their frames became slightly heavier; and the number of wheel spokes increased to six, allowing the wheels to better support the extra weight. The vehicles also became more maneuverable, for their ability to turn as sharply as possible was key to their success in battle.

Because such chariots were very expensive and specialized weapons, the rank of charioteer became highly coveted. Part of an overall transformation of the army into a prestigious profession, this had a significant effect on Egyptian society as well. As Andrea Gnirs puts it:

> Purely military careers were possible and became increasingly frequent, especially in the chariotry; participation in war and possession of a chariot were [equivalent] to prestige and status; as a result, originally military attributes developed into upper-class symbols. . . . A new military [social] class emerged, founded on a new set of social values and a new model of common identity. . . . Now [just] being a soldier sufficed to elicit public respect.[18]

The so-called Stele of Ani, a relief dating from around 1550 to 1086 B.C., shows an Egyptian charioteer and his driver.

Some successful charioteers left behind stories of their adventures. An excerpt from such a tale, on a fourteenth-century B.C. papyrus now in the British Museum, describes a warrior taking his vehicle to a special workshop for repairs:

> They take care of your chariot so that [the wheels are] no longer loose. Your pole is freshly trimmed and its attachments are fitted on. They put bindings on your collar piece . . . and they fix up your yoke. They apply your ensign [personal emblem or symbol], engraved with a chisel, and they put a handle on your whip and attach a lash to it. [Then] you sally forth quickly to fight . . . and accomplish glorious deeds. [19]

The Deadly Composite Bow

The charioteer did not "sally forth" on his vehicle into battle emptyhanded, of course. The role the chariot played in warfare in this age was that of a mobile platform from

A relief dating from around 1403 to 1365 B.C. shows the pharaoh Amenophis III driving his chariot. The long object attached to the side of the vehicle is his bow case.

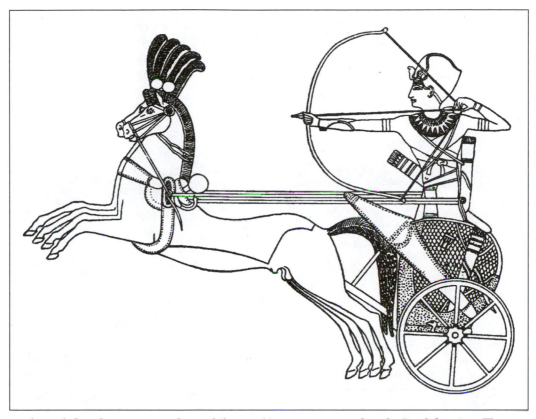

A pharaoh fires his composite bow while attacking an enemy in this idealized drawing. The combination of chariot and composite bow revolutionized warfare.

which a warrior could use various weapons to inflict serious damage on enemy lines. Chief among these chariot-borne weapons was the composite bow, which entered general use in Egypt along with the chariot at the start of the New Kingdom.

Centuries before, probably in Mesopotamia, someone had gotten the bright idea of combining various separate materials to create a bow of greater elasticity and power than the age-old simple version. The four main materials in such a weapon were wood, animal horn, animal tendons (sinew), and glue. Even the wooden portions might be composed of two, three, or four varieties

of wood, each having a certain desired pliability and combined in a carefully planned fashion. The harder animal horn was used in spots that needed more rigidity; and the sinews were applied to the back of the bow to increase its propulsive (springing) power.

The result was a bow that could fire an arrow up to six or seven hundred yards (i.e., six or seven times the length of a football field!), though any sort of accuracy could be maintained only up to about three hundred yards. Still, this was far superior to the performance of an ordinary bow. Composite bows required considerable expertise and expense to make and much practice to use

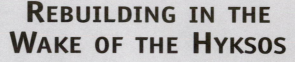

REBUILDING IN THE WAKE OF THE HYKSOS

One of the highlights of the immediate post-Hyksos era of the New Kingdom was the rule of a strong, ambitious woman, Hatshepsut. Daughter of Pharaoh Thutmose I and wife of her half-brother, Thutmose II, from 1473 to 1458 B.C., she was regent and coruler of Egypt with her stepson, Thutmose III. Among Hatshepsut's achievements was the rebuilding of temples and other structures ruined by the Hyksos, as she boasts in this temple inscription (quoted in volume 2 of J.H. Breasted's Ancient Records of Egypt).

A bust of Queen Hatshepsut, who ruled Egypt alongside Thutmose III.

Hear you, all persons! You people as many as you are! I have done this according to the design of my heart. . . . I have restored that which was ruins, I have raised up that which was unfinished since the Asiatics [the Hyksos] were in the midst of Avaris of the Northland, and the barbarians were in the midst of them, overthrowing that which was made, while they ruled in ignorance of [i.e., did not recognize] Ra [the Egyptian sun god].

effectively; so it is not likely that every archer in the Egyptian army had one. Probably charioteers and selected foot archers wielded this special weapon while the rest of the archers carried traditional simple bows.

The widespread use of composite bows fired by warriors either on chariots or on foot inevitably created a need for some way to protect the archers and other soldiers against these missiles. Because firing a bow required both hands, it was too awkward for the archer to hold a large shield; and adding a shield-bearer to the

chariot, which already had an archer and a driver, increased the weight and decreased the agility of the vehicle. The solution, therefore, was the adoption of body armor. Sculptures and paintings from Egypt, Palestine, the island of Cyprus, and elsewhere in the Near East from this period show armored outfits made of copper or bronze scales sewn or glued to leather or linen jerkins. Often attached to the top of such a "mail" suit was a metal tube that protected the neck, chin, and mouth; a metal helmet protected the head.

Weaponry Old and New

The charioteers with their composite bows did not ride into battle alone. They were often the centerpiece of an army and a large-scale attack, but they always acted in concert with traditional infantry (foot soldiers), including foot archers and soldiers wielding axes, swords, and so forth. This gave Egypt somewhat of an advantage over many of the enemies it faced in Syria-Palestine during the New Kingdom. Most of these states relied more on chariotry than infantry because their populations were smaller; whereas, relative to her opponents, as Healy explains,

> Egypt's large population allowed the deployment of a large infantry force; and the experience of centuries in the organization and discipline of large bodies of men [in both military campaigns and large building projects like the pyramids] translated themselves naturally to the army. [20]

As for the makeup of Egyptian infantry units, thanks to the increased professionalism and prestige of the military many native Egyptians filled the ranks. Foreign-born fighters were still important, though, manning large ethnic auxiliary units. These included the traditional Nubian units, including skilled Nubian scouts known as Medjay; Libyans; Palestinians who had been captured and forced to fight for Egypt; and the Sherdan, another captured enemy, who may have originated in Asia Minor (what is now Turkey) and who began fighting in Egyptian armies in the thirteenth century B.C.

The weapons these troops used were a mix of traditional and new. The mace was abandoned because it was not very effective against the mail armor and metal helmets

A surviving specimen of a khopesh, *or "sickle sword." The outer edge was sharpened so that the user could slash outward in a circular stroke.*

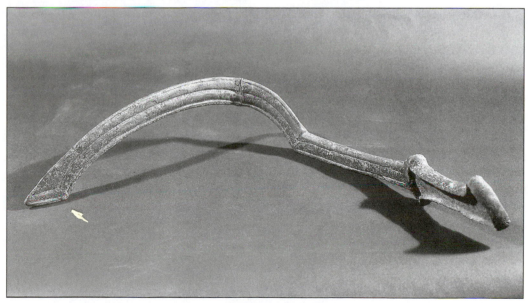

In a relief found at Karnak, the pharaoh Seti I, holding a sickle sword, charges through ranks of Libyan foot soldiers, many of whom lie mortally wounded.

now worn by many troops. But battle-axes were still common because they could pierce most helmets; and spears and javelins remained mainstay infantry weapons. Besides the composite bow, the most effective newer weapon was the *khopesh,* a sword introduced into Egypt from Palestine. The *khopesh,* or "sickle sword," was so named because its curved blade resembled the sickles used to cut wheat, except that the sword blade was much smaller. Also, its outer edge was sharpened, rather than its inner one (as in the case of a normal sickle), and it was made of bronze, a harder metal than copper; these two factors combined to make the *khopesh* a very effective slashing weapon. It was so effective, in fact, that the pharaohs adopted it as the symbol of their authority in place of the mace.

Chariots and Infantry Work Together

The Egyptian infantry could and sometimes did act on its own. But more often, at least in larger pitched battles, commanders used it to support offensive units of chariots. Unfortunately, no descriptions of specific tactics in such battles have survived from the early New Kingdom. But Vanderbilt University scholar Robert Drews provides this plausible reconstruction of a chariot battle of the period:

> [The] opposing chariot forces would hurtle towards each other . . . the squadrons maintaining an assigned order and the archers beginning to discharge their arrows as soon as the enemy came within range (perhaps

KEEPING NUBIA IN LINE

In addition to the considerable attention paid to Syria-Palestine by early New Kingdom pharaohs in the wake of the expulsion of the Hyksos, several of these rulers launched campaigns into Nubia. This account (quoted in volume 2 of Breasted's Ancient Records of Egypt*) from an inscription found at Aswan, Egypt, describes Thutmose II (reigned 1492–1479 B.C.) quelling a Nubian rebellion.*

Then his majesty dispatched a numerous army into Nubia on his first occasion of a campaign, in order to overthrow all those who were rebellious against his majesty or hostile to the Lord of the Two Lands. Then this army of his majesty overthrew those barbarians; they did not let live anyone among their males, according to all the command of his majesty, except one of those children of the chief of wretched Nubia, who was taken away alive as a living prisoner with their people to his majesty. . . . This land was made a subject of his majesty as formerly, [and] the people rejoiced [and] the chiefs were joyful.

A pharaoh rides into battle against the Nubians in this painting found on a chest in King Tutankhamen's tomb.

at a distance of two hundred meters [660 feet] or more). The archers must have shot ever more rapidly and vigorously as the opposing forces closed the distance between them. Of course, many horses were killed or wounded. The whole point of the battle . . . was to bring down as many of the opponent's chariots as possible. . . . After the surviving teams had made their way past each other, the archers may have faced the rear of their vehicles and fired once or twice at their opponents as they receded. Then the two forces, if they were still cohesive, must have wheeled around and begun their second charge, this time from the opposite direction.[21]

Meanwhile, groups of foot soldiers, or "runners," followed the chariots into the fray. Their tasks were to clear the field of capsized chariots, capture or kill fallen enemy archers, and rescue their own fallen bowmen and charioteers. They also attacked or chased after any infantrymen supporting the enemy chariots. Whenever possible, especially in the opening stages of a battle, the runners must have placed themselves behind the chariots, tiny islands of protection in a chaotic sea of flying arrows.

Victory at Megiddo

Despite the absence of detailed contemporary battle descriptions, large numbers of Egyptian inscriptions describe military campaigns in which chariot charges, infantry encounters, and sieges took place. In several of these forays, Egyptian armies entered Syria-Palestine. Perhaps the most vivid, if not the

most important, was the attack on Megiddo by Thutmose III. Thutmose, who reigned from 1479 to 1425 B.C., is sometimes called the Egyptian Alexander the Great, after the famous ancient Greek conqueror, for expanding Egypt's sphere of influence to its largest extent (about 400,000 square miles, almost twice the size of the state of Texas).

Most of Thutmose's immediate predecessors had maintained their influence and dominance over the petty kingdoms of Syria-Palestine. But shortly before he ascended the throne, the powerful kingdom of Mitanni, situated northeast of Syria, had managed to impose its own will on these states. To put down this "rebellion" against Egyptian authority, around 1457 B.C. the pharaoh marched northeast with a large army. Upon reaching northern Palestine, he learned that the enemy host was using the city of Megiddo (the biblical Armageddon) as its base. The daring Thutmose decided to attempt to surprise his opponents by taking his own troops through a narrow, dangerous mountain pass leading directly onto the plain near the city.

This gamble paid off. The Egyptians exited the pass in darkness to find the army of Mitanni encamped less than half a mile away, near the city's walls. According to Thutmose's official annals, just before dawn

[the] command was given to the whole army, saying: "Equip yourselves! Prepare your weapons! for we shall advance to fight with that wretched foe in the morning!" . . . The watch[men] of the army went about, saying, "Steady of heart! Steady of heart! Watchful! Watchful!

Thutmose III, the famous imperialist who expanded Egypt's borders to their greatest extent. In 1457 B.C., he captured the city of Megiddo, in Palestine.

Watch for life at the tent of the king." One [officer] came to say to his majesty, "The land is well and the infantry of the north and south likewise [i.e., it appears that we are in a favorable position for battle]."[22]

At first light, before the surprised enemy could prepare properly, the pharaoh led a frontal assault.

Early in the morning, behold, command was given to the entire army to move. His majesty went forth in a chariot of electrum [an alloy of gold and silver], arrayed in his weapons of war, like [the god] Horus, the Smiter, lord of power. . . . The southern wing of this army of his majesty was at the northwest of Megiddo while his majesty was in their center. . . . Then his majesty prevailed against them at the head of his army.[23]

The charge of the Egyptian chariots and other forces must have been devastating, for the opposing troops "fled headlong to Megiddo in fear, abandoning their horses and their chariots of gold and silver." The rout was so complete that the fleeing soldiers accidentally locked out both the king of Megiddo and the ruler of Kadesh, another local city that had sided with Mitanni. In an embarrassing display, "the people [of Megiddo] hauled them up . . . by their clothing into the city." Thutmose then laid siege to Megiddo for seven months, at which point it surrendered. "The fear of his majesty had entered [their hearts]," his annals conclude, "their arms were powerless, [and] his serpent diadem [crown] was victorious among them. Then were captured their horses, their chariots of gold and silver . . . [and] their champions lay stretched out like fishes on the ground."[24]

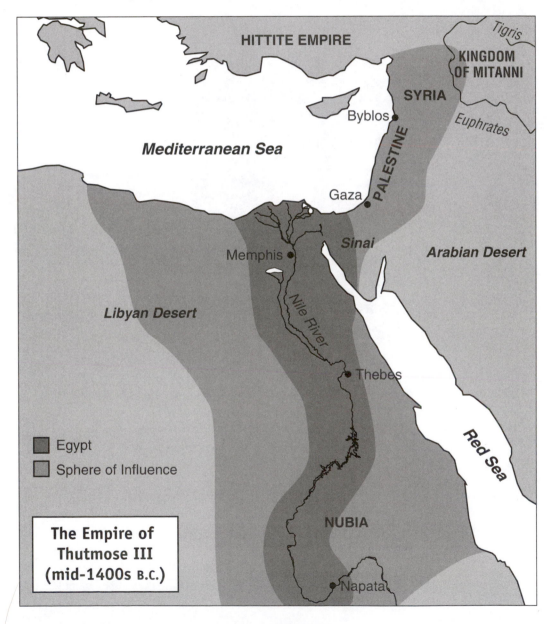

One Threat Recedes, Another Appears

Thutmose followed up his victory by carrying back to Egypt the sons of some thirty-six local rulers and holding them hostage; this ensured that their fathers would remain loyal to Egypt rather than Mitanni. Over the course of years, these young men were indoctrinated with Egyptian ideas and customs and sent back to their home cities to become puppet rulers friendly to Egypt.

Eventually, Thutmose carried the war directly into Mitanni itself. But this campaign was inconclusive; and a generation later, Egypt and Mitanni made peace. After that, Mitanni was never again a serious threat to Egypt. But the latter's troubles as an imperial power were far from over, for far to the north, in the heart of Asia Minor, a new, very formidable empire was rising ominously; in the fullness of time, Hatti, land of the Hittites, would test the Egyptian military's strength and resolve more severely than ever.

CHAPTER THREE

Military Service and Organization

Of the numerous military reliefs and inscriptions commissioned by the pharaohs of the New Kingdom, a good many follow a familiar formula. The king is portrayed as the

Warrior pharaohs often associated themselves in art with the sun god, Ra.

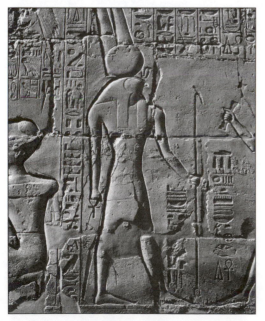

mighty personification of the sun god, Ra (or Re), or else the war god, Montu; he fearlessly leads his army into battle and vanquishes his enemies, glorifying both himself and Egypt. In examining such artifacts, it is sometimes easy to forget that a war leader is usually only as good as the officers and troops he commands. Beneath the supreme, almost godlike position of pharaoh ranged a hierarchy of generals, scribes, unit commanders, charioteers, scouts, weapons and armor makers, and ordinary foot soldiers, all working together in a complex, smoothly running military organization.

A Society Transformed by Soldiering

The army these men served in was largely full time and professional, so they often stayed on for long hitches; and their lives, needs, and deeds became a major facet of Egyptian society. The effects of military preparedness and warfare on the country can be seen on both an individual level and a more general one. For the individual sol-

A poor farmer plows the fields in this surviving painting. In the New Kingdom, a new class of farmers arose, consisting of ex-soldiers.

dier, military service was often hereditary. Once in the army, his name was recorded on lists that were maintained from one generation to the next; and when he retired, or died in action, his son took his place. The son received all the benefits earned by his father, including the use of a plot of land and all slaves who worked on the property. (Soldiers did not actually own such land plots until the thirteenth century B.C.)

On a wider, societal level, the institution of a standing army altered the traditional breakdown of social classes and created the opportunity for upward mobility. In ages past, the vast majority of Egyptians had been dirt-poor peasants working on small farms or government building projects. Most of their labor had benefited a tiny

elite group of rich nobles and priests; the latter owned all the land and there was no substantial middle class. In the New Kingdom, by contrast, in areas where many soldiers and ex-soldiers settled, whole villages emerged in which ordinary men supervised or owned land but did not work it themselves, the actual labor being done by slaves or hired labor. These farmers, small but not poor, Sheikh 'Ibada al-Nubi explains,

represent the birth of an intermediate social group, between the ruling class and those workers who did not possess the means of production. The "middle class" tone of the Eighteenth Dynasty [1550–1295 B.C.], which

Increasing social mobility allowed Horemheb, depicted in this tomb painting, to rise from the position of scribe to occupy Egypt's throne as pharaoh.

was proud of well-made objects displaying a simple good taste and a certain gaiety, is partly due to this nucleus of people exempt from daily work and with a modest, but sufficient income. . . . The existence of a regular army thus profoundly modified the economic structure of the country by encouraging the long-term creation of small and medium-sized property owners, alongside the land owned by the sovereign, princes, and . . . temples. [25]

Significantly, the emergence of this small but important middle class made it possible for at least some ordinary Egyptians to better their lives, as well as those of their children and grandchildren. A middle-class soldier who had not been born of a noble family could now aspire to higher social position, as illustrated by the case of Horemheb. He began as a military scribe and eventually rose through the ranks to become pharaoh, reigning from 1323 to 1295 B.C. Other pharaohs who began their careers in the military ranks included Horemheb's predecessor, Ay (1327–1323 B.C.), and successor, Rameses I (1295–1294 B.C.).

The Top Military Commanders

The position of pharaoh, which Horemheb and a few others attained by hard work rather than aristocratic privilege, represented the pinnacle of Egypt's military organization and administration. A large portion of the youth of a pharaoh-to-be was devoted to learning the military arts, from weapons use to strategy and tactics. This was necessary because as supreme commander the pharaoh did not remain behind in his capital and let his generals run a war, as in the case of the U.S. president and other modern national leaders. "In war

the pharaoh assumed total control of the army on a campaign," Mark Healy writes,

> Not only did this entail him defining the strategy and plan of a campaign but also his personal involvement on the field of battle. [The New Kingdom pharaohs] Thutmose III, Amenhotep II, and Rameses II were all renowned for their leadership of their chariot corps in battle, and their personal bravery seems never to have been in question.[26]

Thus, the fortunes of the country rested in large measure on the personal abilities and

---

A PHARAOH'S PROPAGANDA

As the supreme leaders of the Egyptian army, New Kingdom pharaohs regularly bragged of their military deeds. This is part of a hymn (quoted in volume 2 of Breasted's Ancient Records of Egypt*) inscribed on a marker stone on which the pharaoh Thutmose III is accompanied by a goddess who has supposedly helped ensure his recent victory. Such words and images were effective propaganda designed not only to glorify the king, but also to enhance the image of the army and military service.*

I have worked a marvel for you;
I have given to you might and victory against all countries,
I have set your fame, even the fear of you in all lands.
Your terror [is known] as far as the four pillars of heaven;
I have magnified the dread of you in all bodies,

I have put the roaring of your majesty among the Nine Bows.
The chiefs of all countries are gathered in your grasp,
I myself have stretched out my two hands,
I have bound them for you.
I have bounded together the Nubian troglodytes by tens of thousands and thousands,
[And] the Northerners by hundreds of thousands as captives.
I have felled your enemies beneath your sandals,
You have smitten the hordes of rebels . . . as I commanded you.
The [peoples of the] earth in its length and breadth, Westerners and Easterners [alike], are subject to you,
You trample all countries, your heart glad.

An officer addresses a group of military recruits in the top panel of this New Kingdom painting. A complex chain of command existed in the Egyptian army.

judgment of a single individual. Luckily for Egypt, a majority of the rulers of the New Kingdom were extremely responsible, capable leaders; and a few, most notable among them Thutmose III, can be described as gifted.

Ranked directly beneath the pharaoh were a number of major field commanders. If the pharaoh had a son old enough, the son held the rank of commander in chief and answered only to his father. Next came two chief deputies, each in charge of one of the two sections in which the army was divided in the early New Kingdom—the Northern

Corps, based at Memphis, and the Southern Corps, based at Thebes. After the reign of Horemheb, there were four main army divisions, each composed of roughly five thousand men and commanded by a general. A general maintained his local military base, trained new recruits, prepared his corps for an upcoming campaign, and led that corps on the march.

Each of these small armies—called Amun, P-Re (or Re), Ptah, and Seth (or Sutekh)— was named for an important god associated with the region where it was based. When on campaign, each was a self-contained unit featuring infantry, chariots, and a supply train. They could be combined into one large army for a battle if necessary; or they could work separately to accomplish individual tasks, giving the overall strike force great flexibility. For safety's sake, the four armies did not march through enemy territory together, but rather moved along separated from one another by a distance of about six miles, while messengers on horses or chariots sped among them to maintain communications. "The logic of this organization is apparent," Healy points out,

> given that the principal tactic of the opposition was the employment of skirmishing chariotry to strike at an advancing army on the march. The short distance between each corps ensured that in the event of the protecting chariots of one being swept away, support could be moved forward

quickly to help the infantry now under attack.[27]

Army Scribes and Their Duties

Under the generals were other officers, including standard-bearers, in charge of maintaining and carrying the army's standards (plaques, flags, carvings, and other official symbols), and various deputies. One of the most important ranking positions was that of scribe. There was one main scribe for the entire military, who reported either directly to the pharaoh or to his vizier, a high-ranking nonmilitary official who more or less ran the country for the king. In addition, numerous lower-ranking scribes worked in each of the four army divisions. The scribes had several essential duties without which the army, or any army for that matter, simply could not operate. These included keeping up-to-date lists of all recruits, retirees, deceased, and

A military scribe's duties included keeping lists of new recruits and soldiers who had died in battle.

wounded; ordering, maintaining, and cataloging stocks of supplies; assessing labor needs and assigning workers to address such needs; and dividing rations and equipment among the officers and soldiers. An inkling of the nature of such rations and equipment comes from a surviving scribal order to make preparations for a campaign in Syria:

And further: may you give your attention to have someone equip the . . . horse-team which is destined for Kharu, together with their stablemasters, and likewise their grooms, their "bags of hairy fabric" being filled with fodder and straw . . . their haversacks [packs] being filled with loaves of bread, the asses being individually in the charge of two men [i.e., every two men had one donkey to carry their supplies], [and] their chariots . . . filled with all manner of weapons of war.[28]

Army Units and Foreign Auxiliaries

Finally, there were junior officers who commanded individual units of soldiers. The exact breakdown and sizes of army units are not precisely known, but roughly speaking those smaller than an army division of 5,000 men appear to have been as follows: a host, made up of 500 men; a company, having 250 men (so that there were two companies to a host); a platoon, with 50 men (a company having five platoons); and a squad, with 10 men (a platoon breaking down into five squads). Each unit commander had his own designation; for

A HARDWORKING ARMY SCRIBE

This is part of the often-quoted Satirical Letter (quoted in Alan Shulman's Military Rank, Title, and Organization in the Eyptian New Kingdom*), in which an army scribe named Hori responds to a colleague who is skeptical that Hori works very hard. In somewhat overdramatic terms, Hori describes some of the problems he has faced on the job.*

The keen scribe, skilled of heart, there is nothing about which he does not know. Oh torch in the darkness at the head of the soldiers! . . . You [the scribe] are sent on a mission to Djahi at the head of the victorious soldiers in order to trample down those rebels. . . . What had been brought to you [by the supply depot back in Egypt] is the ration which is before you, namely loaves of bread, small animals, and jars of wine, but the number of people [you have to feed with these supplies] is too large for you, [and] the supply is too small for them! . . . You receive [these supplies] and they are placed in the camp. The soldiers are ready and prepared [to eat]. [Divvy up] the rations in portions, quickly, [placing] that of each man [in] his hands. . . . Oh sapient [wise] scribe, midday has come and the camp is hot. It is time to start [the day's march]. Don't make the [troop commander] angry [by dragging your feet]. Many are the marches before us. . . . Our night quarters are far off.

example, a platoon leader was a "chief of fifty."

There were also Egyptian officers who commanded the groups of foreign auxiliaries who fought in the army. Appropriately, these commanders were called "leaders of foreign troops," and their junior officers, who seem to have been non-Egyptians drawn directly from the foreign ranks, were the "leaders of tribesmen." In ancient sculptures and paintings, scholar Alan R. Shulman points out, these foreign soldiers

> are usually shown in their native dress, equipped with the weapons characteristic of their nations. Only occasionally are they shown in Egyptian dress. . . . They seem to have been always infantry. . . . When not on active duty, the auxiliaries, like the Egyptian troops, were quartered in their own settlements . . . with their weapons stored in government arsenals. This would mean that they were not continuously standing under arms; and consequently that they were not always on active service [and therefore could not pose a threat to Egyptian society as the armed Hyksos had].[29]

Benefits and Drawbacks of Military Service

For the soldiers who fought in these various units, military service had its benefits and drawbacks, as has been true in armies throughout the ages. Egyptian troops (and perhaps on occasion some foreign troops) could look forward to various incentives for enlistment and rewards for service. Besides

the real chance for advancement through the ranks (a privilege probably not granted to foreign troops) and government grants of land on retirement, there was booty. After capturing an enemy camp or town, the pharaoh usually gained large caches of gold, jewels, fine fabrics, horses, slaves, and so forth; and he shared a certain amount of this treasure with his troops. It was also common custom for commanders to allow a soldier to keep as slaves any prisoners he had personally captured. Marching in the pharaoh's victory parade in front of thousands of cheering countrymen was another perk. A relief found at Karnak, the great temple complex at Thebes, shows the Pharaoh Seti I and his army being greeted on their return from an Asiatic campaign. The inscription reads:

> Prophets, nobles, and officials of the South and North, coming to acclaim to the Good God [i.e., the pharaoh], at his return from the country of Retenu [Syria] with very numerous captivity [prisoners]. Never was seen the like of it. . . .They say, in praising his majesty, in magnifying his might: "Welcome are you, from the countries which you have subdued; you are triumphant, and your enemies are beneath you. . . .Your sword was in the midst of every land, and their chiefs fell by your blade.[30]

On the other hand, everyday life for most soldiers—especially on campaigns, which were frequent—was difficult. Typical were long marches through barren regions; extended periods living in squalid conditions far from home and family; numerous camp

GENEROUS RATIONS
FOR THE TROOPS

When the government supplied the troops with sufficient food and other necessary goods, their morale was naturally higher. In this inscription, from the sixth year of the reign of Seti I (ca. 1288 B.C.), the pharaoh is generous to a thousand soldiers sent to procure large blocks of sandstone for a temple he is building (as quoted in volume 3 of J.H. Breasted's Ancient Records of Egypt).

His majesty increased that which was furnished to the army in ointment, ox-flesh, fish, and plentiful vegetables without limit. Every man among them had 20 deben [just under four pounds] of bread daily, bundles of vegetables, a roast of flesh; and linen garments monthly. Thus they worked with a loving heart for his majesty. . . . [The king's messenger and standard-bearers also received] wine, sweet oil, honey, and figs . . . every day.

duties, including large doses of backbreaking work; the increased chance of catching various diseases; and harsh discipline. Quite a few texts have survived, warning young men about the rigors of military life, including this one:

Come, I will speak to you of the ills of the infantryman. . . . He is awakened [before dawn] when there is still an hour left for sleeping. He is driven like a jackass and he works until the sun sets beneath its darkness of night. He hungers and his belly aches. He is dead while he lives. When he receives the grain-ration [he is granted a short rest period] but it [the grain] is not pleasant, for it has been ground. . . . His marches are high in the hills [where trails are narrow, steep, and dangerous], and he drinks only water for three days. It is foul-tasting, like the taste of salt, and his belly is pierced with dysentery. The enemy comes and surrounds him with arrows. . . .

but they [the commanders] say, "Hurry! Forward, oh mighty infantryman! Bring back a good name for yourself!". . . [But] his knee is weak and his face is miserable. . . . [He is forced to carry on his back foreign captives who are too worn out to walk any farther]. His pack is cast away and others seize it. . . . His wife and children are in their village, but he is [either] dead and does not reach it, [or] if he is a survivor, he is [too] exhausted from marching [to enjoy it].[31]

As for military discipline, a number of texts or fragments thereof have survived that describe harsh and exacting punishments for officers and troops alike. Under Horemheb, for instance, there was a rule stating that "if any officer is guilty of extortions or thefts, the law shall be executed against him, in that his nose shall be cut off."[32] The following text describes an offense committed by soldiers—the theft of cattle and other goods belonging to the state:

The two divisions of troops which are in the field, one in the southern region, the other in the northern region, stole hides in the whole land . . .without applying the brand of the royal house to cattle which were not due to them, thereby increasing their number, and stealing that which was stamped from them. They went out from house to house, beating and plundering without leaving a hide for the people. [33]

Those caught received this penalty, also prescribed by Horemheb:

As for any citizen of the army, [about] whom one shall hear, saying: "He goes about stealing hides," beginning with this day, the law shall be executed against him by beating him a hundred blows [with a whip?], opening five wounds, and taking from him by force the hides which he took. [34]

Buying into the Glories of War

One would think that, reading about the privations, tough discipline, and harsh punishments of military life, no one would ever want to join the pharaoh's army. However, the fact is that most ordinary Egyptians could not read and only heard such dire accounts third- or fourthhand by word of mouth. More importantly, the government compensated for these warnings by issuing extremely effective propaganda about the glories of war and serving in the military. "Visible to everyone," al-Nubi points out,

detailed images on the outside walls and forecourts of temples depicted each stage of the military exploits of the king. . . . These representations were copied at different times and in different places. . . . They show the battle's dramatic moments, the deployment of soldiers . . . and the geographical features of the battlefield. . . . The actual facts of the war are used to stimulate the imagination [of the viewers]. [35]

Egyptian foot soldiers march during a military campaign in this carved relief.

As in many lands in all ages, inexperienced, idealistic young men often became infatuated with the image of the soldier running roughshod over a fearful enemy and marching home in a blaze of glory. Once conscripted or enlisted, they learned that there was less glory and much more dirty work and danger involved. But most of those who survived and made it home in one piece reaped sufficient material benefits to make the experience worthwhile and to pass on their proud military mantle to the next eager generation.

CHAPTER FOUR

Borders, Fortifications, and Sieges

The earliest Egyptian fortresses were fortified cities within the country itself. A surviving fragment of a pottery model of a city wall dating back to the Predynastic Period seems to show two soldiers manning a crenellated wall. (Crenellation consists of alternating stone notches and open spaces, a familiar feature of battlements and castles in ancient and medieval times; archers and other soldiers hid behind the protective notches and fired their weapons through the open spaces.) Such defenses were common for cities across the Near East in the fourth and third millennia B.C., an era when neighboring city-states often attacked one another.

In Egypt's case, episodes of warfare between its original two predynastic kingdoms probably necessitated fortifying the walls of important cities. When Menes united those kingdoms about 3100 B.C., initiating the Early Dynastic Period, his new capital, Memphis, was heavily fortified, as reflected in the name he gave it—the White Wall. Later, during the civil wars of the First Intermediate Period, many towns had walls with crenellated battlements. Numerous skulls riddled with cracks and dents, which were discovered in a mass grave at Deir el-Bahari (across the Nile from Thebes), are likely the remains of soldiers trying to scale such walls.

Apart from fortified towns, early on the Egyptians built military forts, mainly along the frontiers between Egypt and foreign territories. These outposts were deemed necessary in the Old and Middle Kingdoms partly because of the long-held view that maintaining the borders was integral to the safety and well-being of the nation. Later, in the New Kingdom, while some Egyptian troops manned these forts in a defensive role, others assumed an offensive posture by following their pharaohs across the borders to lay siege to enemy towns.

These defensive and offensive operations depended on technology and methods that played off of and stimulated each other. When someone invented a new siege device that could breach one part of a fortress, the

The characteristic notches and spaces of crenellation, seen in forts and fortifications through the ages, grace the battlements of an ancient Egyptian fortress.

defenders soon contrived a new strategy or device to counteract the threat; then, the besiegers came up with another innovation, followed by a countermeasure by the defenders; and so forth. Thus, as noted classical scholar Peter Connolly points out, "Fortifications and siege warfare are inextricably [inescapably] combined. The development of one inevitably stimulates changes in the other," [36] and therefore the two must be considered together.

Protecting the Flow of Trade Goods

The three main areas in which the Egyptians erected fortification walls and forts were the Palestinian frontier east of the Nile Delta, the Libyan frontier west of the delta, and the Nubian frontier in the south, at and beyond the region of the First Cataract. (The cataracts are points where the river passes through rocky areas with heavy rapids; these areas were not navigable, so goods had to be downloaded from ships, carried overland, then reloaded onto other ships in the next passable stretch.) The walls and forts in the Nubian frontier are the best preserved in Egypt, and their physical layout is likely representative of examples elsewhere.

The first permanently occupied Egyptian outpost in the Nubian frontier was erected at Buhen, near the Second Cataract, in the mid–third millennium B.C. at the height of the Old Kingdom. The outpost consisted of a small settlement protected by a large stone wall. Evidence shows that copper-smelting was the main activity in the settlement, which reflects the fact that Egypt's primary interest in Nubia was the exploitation of raw materials. Military expansion into the area, which began in earnest in the Middle Kingdom, was designed to protect and maintain the northward flow of valuable goods. Between about 1970 to 1840 B.C., a long chain of forts grew up between Aswan, at the First Cataract, and Buhen, at the Sec-

ond Cataract. These served as both military outposts and customs stations. The Egyptians wanted to make sure that goods moved along smoothly, but at the same time they sought to limit the free flow of "wretched" Nubians into Egypt, as revealed by an inscription on a marker stone set up by the pharaoh Senusret III about 1866 B.C.:

> [The southern boundary of the realm is hereby marked] in order to prevent that any black Nubian should cross it, by water or by land, with a ship or

A heavily weathered and eroded wall in the Buhen fortress, near the Second Cataract, is pierced by several holes through which defenders fired missiles at attackers.

any herds [of livestock belonging to] the black Nubians, except a black Nubian . . . with a commission [i.e., written contract from the Egyptian government]. Every good thing shall be done with them, but without allowing a ship of black Nubians to pass by Semna, going downstream forever.[37]

Clearly, the military forts erected in this period ensured that Egypt would maintain its monopoly on gold and other metals, ivory, animals, and slaves derived from Nubia and other African kingdoms lying farther south. That they were seen as important installations is demonstrated by the high rank of the officer in charge of each. Called a "fort officer," his military position was apparently on a par with the commander of a host; in addition, he seems also to have been a high-ranking administrator reporting directly to the pharaoh's vizier. Evidence sug-

gests that the second in command of a fort was an officer with the title of "scribe of the fort."

Physical Layout of Forts

The forts these men oversaw all had rather similar basic ground plans. Each was built around a convenient grid of narrow streets lined by storerooms, workshops, barracks for the soldiers, and larger quarters for the officers. A wider street encircled the complex on the inside of the defensive wall, allowing the residents easy access to the battlements in an emergency. Most of the forts were erected near the Nile and had protected walkways or tunnels leading to the river so as to ensure an ample supply of fresh water in case of siege.

The fortification walls and battlements that surrounded such military camps were large, impressive, and designed to repel large-scale attack (although it is unclear how often the Nubians were able to mount

SOME ODDLY SHAPED FORTS

Although the basic inner layout of most Egyptian Middle Kingdom forts was the same—a grid of narrow streets lined by buildings—the shapes of the outer defensive walls of these structures sometimes varied, as explained by Ian Shaw in his Egyptian Warfare and Weapons.

The Middle Kingdom forts . . . were probably designed by only one or two architects, [yet] they show fascinating variations in response to the local topography. Whereas the two largest sites, Buhen and

Mirgissa, were simply rectangular structures (as were all five of the surviving forts north of the Second Cataract group), the rest had idiosyncratic [individual] shapes dictated by the terrain. The fort at Semna, for instance, was built in an L shape in order to conform with the rocky hill on which it stood. At Uronarti, an island near Semna, the fort was triangular in shape and the northern side was more heavily fortified with huge towers, since the flatter terrain to the north made attacks from that direction more dangerous.

This view of the northwest battlements of the Buhen fortress shows a row of square bastions and protruding below them, two semicircular bastions with firing holes.

such assaults). Yigael Yadin provides this more detailed description of the defenses at the largest and best preserved fortress of the Middle Kingdom, at Buhen (which had been much expanded since the Old Kingdom):

> The fortress is almost square, measuring 170 by 180 meters [558 by 590 feet]. The fortifications comprise four basic elements: the main (inner) wall, the outer or advance wall, the moat, and the very well-fortified gate structure. The main wall was built of bricks and was about five meters [16 feet]

thick. It is considered [by experts] to have been 10 meters [32 feet] high. The gate was in the center of the western side of the wall. Throughout its entire length, the wall was "blistered" at intervals of 5 meters with protruding square bastions [large stone barriers], each two meters [6.5 feet] wide. Each corner of the fortress was marked by a large tower, which protruded from the face of the wall even more conspicuously than the bastions. An impressive feature of the Buhen fortifications is the [positioning] and the form of the low outer wall. . . . This

THE WATER SUPPLY AT MEGIDDO

In planning and constructing forts and fortified cities, ancient builders, including the Egyptians and their opponents, inevitably had to consider the problem of the water supply. At all times, but especially when under siege, a fortified settlement needed a ready supply of fresh water, else it could not support its inhabitants for more than a few days. Digging deep wells beneath the settlement or excavating underground tunnels to distant water sources were among the approaches to solving this problem. One of the more formidable examples in the Near East was that of Megiddo, in Palestine, which the pharaoh Thutmose III besieged and captured. The town's water supply was located in an underground cave more than two hundred feet outside the defensive walls. In a Herculean effort, the builders dug a shaft about a hundred feet deep, the same depth of the well, within the city walls; then they excavated a horizontal tunnel from the bottom of the shaft to the well. Cleverly, they made the tunnel's floor slope slightly downward toward the city so that the force of gravity would move the water from one end to the other. Finally, they firmly sealed the cave entrance to the well to make sure that an enemy could not find and destroy the precious water supply.

low wall was also of brick, and along its face a series of semicircular bastions 3 meters [10 feet] wide had been built at intervals of 10 meters. In the wall and the bastion were two rows of firing [holes]. . . . Each enabled fire to be applied downward onto the attackers in the moat in three directions. . . . At the foot of the outer wall there was a dry moat 8.5 meters [28 feet] wide and more than 6 meters [20 feet] deep. To make it even more difficult to cross, an additional low wall had been built on its farther bank.[38]

The gate complex at Buhen is of special interest and shows that the Egyptians were considerably advanced in the art of defensive fortification. On each side of the large, double-doored gate was a tower similar to those occupying the corners of the fortress. These gate towers extended outward for fifteen meters (forty-nine feet), well past the low wall on the outer bank of the moat. Defenders could stand on a crenellated walkway at the top of these towers, so that they overlooked and could fire weapons down onto the area directly in front of the gate. (The need for such elaborate and formidable gate defenses strongly suggests that potential attackers in this era possessed battering rams designed to crash through gates; the regular walls and moat would have been more than sufficient to fend off an assault by arrows, spears, and other handheld weapons.)

Sieges: Erecting an Enclosure Wall

The Egyptians were adept not only at defending their forts against attack, but also at attacking enemy forts and fortified towns. This is attested in numerous surviving inscriptions. For example, the siege of

Megiddo, directed by Thutmose III after his defeat of the army of Mitanni in the early 1400s B.C., was recorded in that pharaoh's annals:

His majesty commanded the officers of the troops to go [forth and besiege the citadel], assigning to each his place. They measured this city, surrounding it with an enclosure, walled about with green timber of all their pleasant trees. His majesty himself was upon the fortification east of this city, inspecting [the work]. . . . It was walled about with a thick wall. . . . Its name was made: "Thutmose III-is-the-Surrounder-of-the-Asiatics." People were stationed to watch over the tent of his majesty, to whom it was said: "Steady of heart!" His majesty commanded [his men], saying "Let not one among them [the confined enemy] come forth outside, beyond this wall, except to come out in order to knock at the door of their fortification [i.e., to signal that they are ready to surrender the city]."[39]

The account mentions an enclosure wall erected around the city, which was obviously intended to prevent any of the defenders

A relief sculpture of Thutmose III, victor at Megiddo. According to Egyptian annals, this was only one of several cities he besieged in Syria-Palestine.

from escaping and also to keep food and/or reinforcements from getting in. The wall was constructed with the wood from "all" the trees in the area. Leveling the surrounding forests was probably designed to eliminate hiding places for any escapees as well as to provide the material needed for the enclosure wall. It was apparently a common technique in Near Eastern sieges in the era of the New Kingdom. The biblical book of Deuteronomy, which originated in Palestine in the latter part of the era, tells besiegers to use the same approach, with the proviso that fruit trees that might feed the attackers should be left undisturbed:

> When you besiege a city for a long time, making war against it in order to take it . . . only the trees which you know are not trees for food you may destroy and cut down that you may build siegeworks against the city that makes war with you, until it falls.[40]

Sieges: Saps and Scaling Ladders

Except for the enclosure wall, the royal account of the Megiddo siege does not mention any specific siege methods or devices the Egyptians employed. However, several surviving Egyptian reliefs illustrating sieges provide such details. A relief found in a tomb in Saqqara, a burial site near Memphis, shows an army of Egyptians methodically assaulting an enemy fortress. Some of the soldiers are in the process of digging a tunnel (or sap) under the walls. Meant either to weaken and collapse the walls or to give access to the citadel, or both, this was a common siege technique throughout ancient and medieval times. While the sappers work, other Egyptians climb scaling ladders that lean against the fortress walls. Significantly, the ladders have wheels at the bottom, indicating that they have been rolled rather than carried into place. The

---

A CAPTURED TOWN YIELDS RICH BOOTY

Using scaling ladders, axes, and other weapons and devices, Egyptian armies captured numerous towns in Syria-Palestine over the centuries; but perhaps no pharaoh breached as many defensive walls as Thutmose III. In this excerpt from his official annals (quoted in volume 2 of J.H. Breasted's Ancient Records of Egypt*), his forces captured the Syrian town of Arvad and collected much booty.*

Behold, his majesty overthrew the city of Arvad, with its grain, cutting down all its pleasant trees. . . . Their gardens were filled with their fruit, their wines were found remaining in their presses as water flows, [and] their grain . . . was more plentiful than the sands of the shore. The [soldiers of the] army were overwhelmed with their [individual] portions [of the booty] . . . [which included] 51 slaves male and female; 30 horses; 10 flat dishes of silver . . . 470 jars of honey; 6,428 jars of wine; [large quantities of] copper [and] lead . . . 616 large cattle; 3,636 small cattle; [many] loaves [of bread] . . . [and] all the good fruit of this country.

In this drawing based on a carved relief, an Egyptian army led by pharaoh Rameses II lays siege to a fortress. The defenders use long poles to push away the scaling ladders.

reliefs show that in such situations, Egyptian archers fired barrages of arrows at the battlements to provide cover for the climbers as they made their way up the ladders.

Other reliefs show attacking Egyptians using battle-axes to chop down wooden fortress gates. Most of these scenes come from the New Kingdom, when the Egyptians no longer, or at least rarely, used the battering ram, which had been a fairly common feature of Old and Middle Kingdom sieges. "The absence of the battering ram in the Egyptian armies of the New Kingdom," Yadin suggests,

may have several explanations: the considerable distance between the military bases in Egypt and the battlegrounds in [Syria-Palestine], which no doubt proved a tough administrative and technical obstacle for the movement of this heavy instrument . . . and more particularly, the firmness of the fortifications at the end of the previous and the beginning of this period. These fortifications were built especially to withstand the battering ram. And they succeeded in blunting its effectiveness, for it was not as yet a perfect instrument. [41]

Greek soldiers climb from their hiding place inside the Trojan Horse in a famous mythological scene. A number of Egyptian accounts tell of similar penetration of city defenses by stealth.

Sieges: The Use of Stealth

Another approach to taking a fortress or fortified town was somehow to trick the besieged into lowering their defensives long enough for the besiegers to gain entry. The most famous version from ancient times was the incident in the Trojan War in which the Greeks pretended to give up their long siege of Troy. They left a huge wooden horse in front of the city and then sailed away. The jubilant Trojans dragged the horse, which they thought was an offering to the gods, into the city, not realizing that a squad of Greek soldiers was hiding in its belly. That night the Greeks crept out, opened the gates for their comrades, who had sneaked back under cover of darkness, and sacked the city.

Although this account is legend rather than fact, it resembles a number of other similar ancient accounts, including some from Egypt. The frequency of references to them suggests that such stratagems of stealth were actually attempted from time to time. Perhaps the most renowned Egyptian version, which predates the Trojan War by two centuries, tells how the pharaoh Thutmose III supposedly captured the city of Jaffa, in Palestine. The Egyptian commander Thot sent a message to the prince of Jaffa, saying that Thot had decided to surrender and would signify his submission by sending gifts in baskets.

> And he [Thot] had the 200 baskets brought . . . and he had 200 soldiers get down into them. And their arms were filled with [weapons and ropes] and they were sealed up with seals [i.e., the baskets were sealed shut with the men inside]. . . . And they had every good soldier carrying them. . . . And they [the carriers, who were unarmed] were told, "When you enter the city, you are to let out your companions and lay hold on all the people who are in the city and put them in bonds immediately."[42]

Thinking that Thot was surrendering, the prince of Jaffa allowed him to enter the city accompanied by the unarmed men carrying the gift baskets. Once inside, the men followed their orders and unsealed the baskets, allowing the armed Egyptians to burst forth and capture the city.

How much of this story is true and how much fable is unknown. What is certain is that the Egyptians of the New Kingdom

In a scene found on a wall of the mortuary temple of Rameses II, the pharaoh and his army are attacking the fortress at Dapur, held by the Hittites.

successfully besieged many fortresses and cities using a wide variety of devices and methods. At the same time, they built many fortresses of their own to control trade routes, guard border areas, and intimidate their enemies. In this way they carved out and maintained a large sphere of influence in the Near East; and for a period of about five hundred years, more than twice as long as the United States has existed, Egypt was unarguably one of the world's great powers.

CHAPTER FIVE

Egypt's Military Zenith: The Battle of Kadesh

The Egyptians fought hundreds of battles in dozens of campaigns stretching over the long years of the Old, Middle, and New Kingdoms. Yet only one battle, perhaps the greatest and most strategic of all, was recorded in any detail in reliefs and inscriptions. The battle of Kadesh (or Qadesh), fought in Syria circa 1274 B.C., was the only Egyptian battle, and also the earliest battle in world history, for which a specific play-by-play account can be reconstructed.

Not surprisingly, given its importance, modern scholars have devoted considerable attention to Kadesh. On the one hand, close examination of the battle reveals vital information about the military tactics the Egyptians employed—how they moved armies through enemy territory, how they utilized scouts and other military intelligence to gather information about enemy forces, how chariots were used to break up troop formations, and how a war leader dealt with reverses on the battlefield and attempted to initiate counteroffensives. On the other hand, the battle represents a significant turning point in the saga of ancient Egypt; this historical moment witnessed the last major high point of both the Egyptian military and the country's imperial sphere of influence.

The Hittites Threaten Syria

That sphere had been carved out by the early pharaohs of the Eighteenth Dynasty, the first of the three dynasties comprising the New Kingdom. The triumphant campaigns of Thutmose III, highlighted by his great victory over Mitanni at Megiddo in 1482 B.C., had been designed to ensure Egypt's permanent control of Syria-Palestine. It was no accident that great Near Eastern powers like Egypt, Mitanni, Assyria, and others coveted the region, particularly the area of Syria. As Mark Healy explains:

> During this period, Syria was the crossroads of world commerce. Goods from the Aegean [Sea, bordering Greece's eastern coast] and

These bronze spear and ax heads were made in ancient Syria.

beyond entered the Near East via [Syrian] ports such as Ugarit, whose ships dominated maritime trade in the eastern Mediterranean. Underwater excavations of late Bronze Age ships . . . show the remarkable range of goods they carried—copper, tin, chemicals, tools, glass ingots, ivory . . . jewelry, luxury goods, timber, textiles, and foodstuffs. This merchandise was then distributed throughout the Near East and beyond by a network of extensive trade

routes. From the east and south, these same land routes were used by merchants who brought raw materials such as precious metals . . . and other merchandise from as far afield as Iran and Afghanistan to trade in . . . Syria. With its inherent fertility and richness in natural resources, Syria therefore offered much to predatory powers seeking to use such wealth for their own benefit.[43]

By conquering large portions of Syria, Thutmose ensured that his nation would tap into and exploit the area's wealth and resources. But he faced the same problem that pharaohs both before and after him did, namely, that Syria lay some six hundred miles from Egypt's heartland. This was much too far to facilitate firm Egyptian control for very long without committing thousands of troops and settlers to the region on a permanent basis, a price the Egyptians were unwilling and indeed unable to pay. Luckily for them, the once formidable threat posed by Mitanni receded. A treaty enacted in the reign of Thutmose IV ushered in three generations of peace with that kingdom. But other powers would soon make their own bids for Syrian treasure, creating even bigger threats than Mitanni had.

The first major culprit, from Egypt's viewpoint, was the Hittite empire, centered at Hattusas, in the uplands of north-central Asia Minor. The Hittites had first risen to power in the sixteenth century B.C., at about the time of the founding of Egypt's New Kingdom, and had launched attacks into Mesopotamia and other parts of the Near East. After a brief flurry of activity, they had faded back into obscurity in their homeland. About 1380 B.C., however, the accession of King Suppiluliumas I to Hatti's throne signaled a new burst of Hittite expansion.

This time the Hittites moved south into Syria and southeast into Mitanni. That latter, pressed by the Mesopotamian kingdom of Assyria on one side and the Hittites on the other, buckled. Suppiluliumas drove into Mitanni's heartland and sacked its capital of Washukkanni. The small states and walled cities of Syria—including Aleppo, Ugarit, Carchemish, and Kadesh—now fell to the Hittites one after another.

The response to these events by the last few Eighteenth Dynasty pharaohs was tepid or nonexistent. Only when Seti I, second ruler of the Nineteenth Dynasty, came to the throne did Egypt attempt to reassert itself in Syria. About 1290 B.C. Seti led an army north and defeated the Hittites near Kadesh. "His majesty made a great slaughter," reads an inscription on a relief at Karnak, "smiting the Asiatics, beating down the Hittites, slaying their chiefs . . . charging among them like a tongue of fire!"[44] However, just as Thutmose and others had before, Seti found it difficult to maintain Egypt's influence in a land so far away. The Hittites soon regained control over much of Syria; and the scene was set for the climactic confrontation at Kadesh between Seti's son, Rameses II, and Hatti's new king, Muwatallis.

The Opposing Forces

When Rameses succeeded his father as pharaoh in 1279 B.C., the young man was in his twenties and filled with vigor and ambition. He wished to follow up on Seti's campaign and restore all of Syria to the huge sphere of influence the early New Kingdom pharaohs had maintained in the region. With this goal in mind, in the summer of the fourth year of his reign (ca. 1275 B.C.), he set out with an army, forged his way northward through Palestine, and

RAMESES GATHERS MILITARY INTELLIGENCE

Various surviving Egyptian documents, especially those dealing with the battle at Kadesh, describe the use of military intelligence by Egyptian armies. In this excerpt from Rameses' official account of the Kadesh expedition (quoted in volume 3 of Breasted's Ancient Records of Egypt*), the pharaoh himself questions two Hittite spies in an attempt to confirm the position of the enemy army.*

As his majesty sat upon a throne of gold, there arrived [an Egyptian] scout . . . [who] brought two scouts of [the Hittite king].

They were conducted into the presence [of the pharaoh], and his majesty said to them, "Who are you?" They said, "The [Hittite king] has caused that we should come to spy out where his majesty [the pharaoh] is." Said his majesty to them, "He! Where is he, the [Hittite king]? . . . I have heard he is in the land of Aleppo." Said they, "See, the [Hittite king] . . . [and his army, which is] equipped with infantry and chariotry . . . more numerous than the sands of the shore . . . are standing, drawn up for battle, behind Kadesh the deceitful [i.e., out of your view on the far side of the town]."

captured the Syrian region of Amurru, lying to the southwest of Kadesh. He did not
encounter a Hittite army. And when he returned to Egypt, he was apparently confident that a second campaign the following
year would bring the rest of Syria back
into the Egyptian fold.

King Muwatallis was not so easily intim-
idated, however. He delivered a message to
Rameses announcing a Hittite war declara-
tion and began preparing his forces to meet
the Egyptians near Kadesh. Rameses had to
be genuinely concerned. Though Egyptian
propaganda from this period typically pic-
tured Hittite warriors as effeminate (un-
manly) and Hatti's army as inferior, in
reality Muwatallis's soldiers were formidable fighters and his army easily a match for
that of Egypt.

The differences in style and tactics between these opposing forces had a major
bearing on the events of the impending battle and its outcome. First and foremost, the
Hittites placed a greater emphasis on chariotry than the Egyptians and used it differ-
ently. Whereas Egyptian chariots were
lightweight and carried two men, Hittite
versions were wider, heavier, and carried a
three-man crew. This crew consisted of a
driver, a fighter, and a shield-bearer to protect the fighter. In contrast to an Egyptian
chariot warrior, who wielded a composite
bow and some javelins, his Hittite counter-
part brandished a thrusting spear.

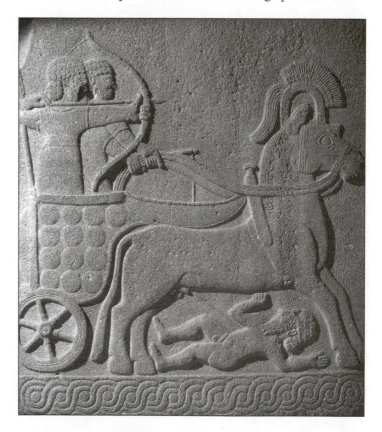

A Hittite king mows down his enemies in this ancient relief. The Hittite Empire, centered in what is now Turkey, challenged Egypt for control of Syria-Palestine.

A RELIEF SCULPTURE
OF THE BATTLE

In this tract from his Collapse of the Bronze Age, *Manuel Robbins describes one of the primary sources of evidence for the battle fought at Kadesh—a relief sculpture at Luxor (a religious complex at Thebes).*

The Kadesh sculpture at Luxor is a masterpiece of composition and clarity. . . . It was necessary to show each of the groups who participated in the battle in such a way that the onlooker would instantly recognize each. While hieroglyphic text accompanied the panorama and explained it, the designers knew that many onlookers would be illiterate. . . . The illustration had to tell the story. . . . In the left center the viewer sees the fortress of Kadesh, with battlements and towers. Around Kadesh, the streams of the Orontes [River] flow. . . . Just outside the fortress [warriors] are assembled, armed . . . with bows, spears, short swords. These warriors are part of the Hittite forces. Distinct nationalities are evident. Hittites can be recognized by their hairstyle . . . Syrians by their long hair, beards, and robes, and other nationalities by long braided hair. . . . In the right center is Rameses in his chariot, facing Kadesh. He is superhuman in size, towering over ordinary mortals. . . . His draw of [his] huge bow is effortless . . . his appearance perfect and god-like. Across the bottom at the left, the Hittite infantry is drawn up, rank upon rank. . . . Forward of them is the Hittite chariotry, charging toward the right and surging around Rameses. . . . At the far left is a figure of larger than ordinary size, yet much smaller than Rameses. . . . His chariot is faced away from the action, as if a quick escape is contemplated. This is how the Egyptians present Muwatallis, the Hittite king. In the center of the composition . . . is a scene of chaotic battle. Hittite chariots and horses are overturned. Bodies, all of them Hittite or Hittite allies, are tumbling through the air. . . . It is a massive slaughter. . . . It is the story in pictures as Rameses wanted it told.

The Egyptians used their chariots as platforms from which to launch their missile weapons at a distance; but the Hittite chariots were a shock force designed to crash headlong into enemy infantry. Once in the fray, the Hittite chariot warriors used their spears to stab at foot soldiers and break up their ranks; then the Hittite infantry attacked and finished off the enemy. (The chief weapons employed by Hittite foot soldiers were much the same as for Egyptian infantry—spears, battle-axes, and sickle swords, by now all fashioned of bronze.)

According to Egyptian sources, King Muwatallis assembled some 37,000 infantrymen and as many as 2,500 chariots— if true an unusually large army in that era. (If these numbers are indeed accurate, they likely included contingents from some of the local vassal states under Hittite control.) To meet this threat, the Egyptians had about 18,000 foot soldiers and perhaps 2,000 chariots. Per usual, the Egyptian army was divided into four large field units—Amun, P-Re, Ptah, and Seth—each of which could act on its own or combine with the others.

The Ruse

At the end of April 1274 B.C., Rameses led these units into Palestine and stopped in the

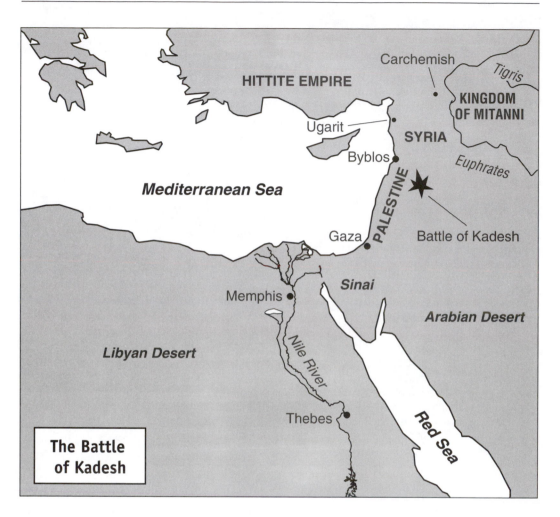

The Battle of Kadesh

area now known as Gaza. There, he divided his forces, sending a small detachment due north with orders to move along the coast, put on a show of force to intimidate the local towns, and meet up with him later at Kadesh. The identity of these troops is unclear and often debated by scholars. Ancient sources call them *Ne'arin,* which translates as "young men" or "recruits." They may have been an elite force drawn from one or more of the four main Egyptian units.[45] Whoever they were, after sending them on their way, the pharaoh continued northward on the usual route taken by Egyptian campaigners in the region—east of the Sea of Galilee and through the Bekáa Valley. Rameses personally led the army of Amun, which was followed by P-Re, Ptah, and Seth, each separated from the others by a few miles, per custom.

Meanwhile, Hatti's ruler had hatched a clever and sinister plan designed to deceive and defeat Rameses. As J.H. Breasted tells it, Muwatallis concealed the bulk of his own army on the northwest side of Kadesh, hidden from the Egyptians by the city. The Hittite king now used the city to mask his movements, and as Rameses pushed northward on the west side of Kadesh, the Hittite commander shifted his position rapidly eastward and southward, all the time keeping the city between him and the advance of the Egyptians. [46]

Next, Muwatallis ordered two local men loyal to him to carry a false message to Rameses. As the pharaoh led Amun through a forest and prepared to cross the Orontes River at a point not far south of Kadesh, he encountered the two men, who claimed:

Our brethren, who belong to the greatest of the families [allied] with the [Hittite king], have made us come to his majesty [i.e., the Egyptian pharaoh], to say: "We will be subjects of Pharaoh, and we will flee from the [Hittite king]; for the [Hittite king] sits [with his army] in the land of Aleppo, on the north of Tunip. He fears [the armed might] of Pharaoh, [and refuses] to come southward." [47]

Rameses fell for the ruse. Reasoning that Aleppo was far to the north and the Hittites well out of range, he led Amun across the

A detail from a large carved relief of the battle at Kadesh, found in Rameses' mortuary temple at Thebes, shows Egyptian arrows devastating Hittite soldiers and horses.

71

Orontes, camped near Kadesh, and prepared to besiege the city.

Charge of the Hittite Chariots

It was sometime in the next few hours that the Egyptians captured two Hittite spies whom Muwatallis had sent to keep watch on Rameses. Under torture, the men revealed the truth—that the Hittite army was lying in wait on the far side of the city and preparing to attack the rear units of the Egyptian army. This unwelcome news surely alarmed Rameses. At that moment P-Re had just crossed the Orontes and was moving, alone and exposed, across the open plain south of Kadesh. Meanwhile, Ptah and Seth were

In this nineteenth-century etching, Rameses, astride his war chariot, heroically pushes his way through the Hittite ranks, killing some and sending others into flight.

still some miles behind in the forest on the far side of the river.

Hoping to warn his unsuspecting troops, the pharaoh dispatched runners. But it was too late. A mass of Hittite chariots suddenly emerged from behind the town, crossed the shallow Orontes, and charged into P-Re's unprotected right flank. Totally unprepared for battle, the Egyptian chariots in that unit were smashed or swept aside by the heavier, fast-moving Hittite vehicles; at the same time, the unit's infantrymen panicked and fled northward toward the camp of Amun. Seeing their comrades approaching at the run, with the enemy chariots in hot pursuit, the troops of Amun also fell into confusion.

At this point, Rameses realized that he had to act quickly to avoid a major defeat. According to the official Egyptian account of the event: "He seized the adornments of battle and arrayed himself in his coat of mail. . . .Then he [went] to his horses, and led [them] quickly on, being alone by himself. He charged into the [forces] of the [Hittite king]."[48] Likely accompanied only by his personal bodyguard of a few chariots and troops, the pharaoh boldly attacked the enemy chariot corps from the side or rear. The lighter Egyptian vehicles, which could turn easier and faster than the Hittite versions, darted in and out, firing arrows and inflicting heavy damage on Muwatallis's surprised men. The general state of confusion now worked in the Egyptians' favor. "In the swirling mêlée," Healy suggests, "it is very possible that the Hittites were not aware of the small size of the force attacking them."[49] Encouraged by Rameses' efforts, many of the other Egyptians began

Rameses smites the Hittites in another relief depicting the battle at Kadesh.

to regroup behind their king, and the tide of battle began to change.

Reinforcements on Both Sides

Now it was Muwatallis's turn to be alarmed. Trying to regain his momentum, he sent another large force of chariots across the river. In all likelihood these fresh troops would have sealed the fate of Rameses and his greatly outnumbered troops. However, as the Hittite reinforcements bore down on the exhausted Egyptians, seemingly out of nowhere the unit of "young men" the pharaoh had earlier sent up the Palestinian coast appeared on the scene. They hurled themselves at the newly arrived Hittite chariots, and soon Rameses joined in the attack, which pushed back and decimated most of these vehicles.

By the end of the day, Rameses had managed to regroup the remnants of P-Re and Amun. King Muwatallis still had forces in reserve; but he broke off his assault, perhaps in part because he learned that fresh troops of Ptah and Seth were rapidly approaching to bolster the Egyptian ranks. The next morning a second confrontation apparently took place near the river south of the city. But like the first stage of the battle, it was largely indecisive.

So Rameses and Muwatallis reluctantly agreed to a temporary peace. Both rulers returned to their countries and claimed victory, though in truth there was no clear winner. Nearly a generation of uneasy

This tablet bears part of the treaty signed about 1259 B.C. between Rameses II and the Hittite king Hattusilis III.

ATTACK AND COUNTERATTACK

This excerpt from an Egyptian account of the encounter at Kadesh (quoted in volume 3 of Breasted's Ancient Records of Egypt*) describes the Hittite attack on the army of P-Re and Rameses' heroic counterattack.*

The [Hittite king] came, and the numerous countries [vassal states] which were with him. They crossed over the channel [Orontes River] on the south of Kadesh and charged into the army of his majesty while they were marching and not expecting it. Then the infantry and chariotry of his majesty retreated before them, northward to the place where his majesty was. . . . When his majesty saw them [the approaching enemy], he was enraged against them, like his father, Montu [the war god]. . . . He seized the adornments of battle, and arrayed himself in his coat of mail. . . . Then he [went] to his horses and led [them] quickly on, being alone by himself. He charged into the [forces] of the [Hittite king] and the numerous countries which were with him. His majesty . . . hurled them headlong, one upon another into the water of the Orontes.

standoffs ensued until about 1259 B.C., when Rameses signed a treaty with a new Hittite king, Hattusilis III. It was without doubt the end of an era, and not only because peace had replaced war; though neither kingdom could foresee it, within half a century both would be in precipitous and irreversible decline. After Kadesh, never again would Egypt launch a major military campaign into Syria or experience the level of international power and influence it had enjoyed for nearly three centuries.

CHAPTER SIX

Warships and the Defeat of the Sea Peoples

The Egyptians had a long tradition of shipbuilding and sailing stretching well back into the Predynastic Period. This is not surprising considering that the Nile was the central focus of the country's inhabited region; and the river served as the principal means of transporting people and goods over long distances. Early on the pharaohs and their generals realized that they could also transport troops more easily over water than over land. Reliefs from the mortuary temple of a Fifth Dynasty king, Sahura, show a fleet of vessels carrying his troops to the coast of Syria-Palestine. Many Middle and New Kingdom rulers used seagoing troop transports to ferry armies to the same region, including the great imperialist Thutmose III.

These boats were not warships in the traditional sense. Most evidence suggests that they did not engage in naval battles with other ships, although they might have on occasion come under fire from hostile forces. For example, the accounts of Ahmose's assault on the Hyksos stronghold of Avaris at the dawn of the New Kingdom mention what appears to have been an amphibious attack in a canal adjoining the town. Probably some small ships or barges ferried troops across the canal, and the defenders on the battlements attempted to stop them with showers of missile weapons.

Not until the reign of Rameses III (ca. 1184–1153 B.C.), near the end of the New Kingdom, do Egyptian sources describe an actual naval battle in which opposing crews of sailors and marines (soldiers trained to fight aboard ships) engage one another. Even then and for a long time afterward, such encounters took place in shallow waters near the Egyptian coast. The Egyptians did not take part in major naval fights far from home until they came under Greek rule many centuries after the close of the New Kingdom.

Traveling Ships and Troop Transports

For more than two thousand years, therefore, Egyptian warships were basically troop transports; and as such they were designed and constructed in essentially the same way as traditional Egyptian boats. In fact, states noted scholar-artist Björn Landström, most of the time

> they were probably ordinary Nile craft of various kinds. Everything from grand traveling ships for kings and captains to simpler transports for ordinary warriors [might be called into service to ferry troops]. . . . The same craft could have many different functions.[50]

Evidence for what such ships looked like and how they were built comes partly from surviving reliefs and paintings. A painting in a tomb at Saqqara dating to circa 2450 B.C. (in the Fifth Dynasty), for instance, shows shipwrights busily constructing a large vessel. There is also Herodotus's account of Egyptian shipbuilding and river navigation. Herodotus was a Greek historian who lived in the fifth century B.C. and traveled to Egypt to study the country and its people firsthand. Although he visited more than five centuries after the end of the New Kingdom, the natives still employed

A well-preserved relief shows Egyptians navigating the Nile River in reed boats. The Nile was the country's main highway throughout antiquity.

Models of Egyptian boats were commonly placed in tombs to symbolize the journey of the deceased to Abydos, center of the cult of Osiris, lord of the dead.

most of the same construction techniques that had been in use since before the advent of the Old Kingdom. Moreover, the kind of vessel Herodotus describes existed in Egypt long before and long after his day. "The Nile boats used for carrying freight," he begins,

> are built of acacia wood. The acacia resembles in form the lotus of Cyrene. . . . They cut short planks, about three feet long, from this tree, and the method of construction is to lay them together like bricks and through-fasten

them with long spikes set close together, and then, when the hull is complete, to lay the deck-beams across on top. The boats have no ribs [although it appears that some Egyptian vessels did have wooden ribs] and are caulked from inside with papyrus [a tough material made from sedge, a water plant that grew in abundance in the Nile Delta]. They are given a single steering-oar, which is driven down through the keel; the masts are of acacia wood, the sails of papyrus. These vessels cannot sail up the river without

TUTANKHAMEN'S SHIPS

Much of what modern scholars know about ancient Egyptian ships comes from studying miniature versions found in the tomb of a short-lived but famous king, as explained here by scholar-artist Björn Landström in his Ships of the Pharaohs.

In the Old Kingdom, at least during certain periods, real ships were placed around the tombs of the kings, some perhaps in the form of sun boats, others as ships of state or royal ships. . . . It is probable that the kings of the New Kingdom had with them only models of their royal ships, one rigged for voyages up the Nile, the other unrigged. Only the Tomb of Tutankhamen [popularly known as King Tut, who reigned from ca. 1336–1327 B.C.] has been preserved intact until our time, and this contained such models, together with a large number of other model traveling vessels, perhaps intended for the royal court. Unlike almost everything else in the tomb of Tutankhamen, these models are not particularly well executed and seem to have been made in great haste after the king's death. The hull decoration has clearly been done in a hurry. . . . Even so . . . these models provide a wealth of interesting details.

This model ship, which shows minute details of construction, was found in the tomb of the boy-pharaoh, Tutankhamen ("King Tut").

a good leading wind, but have to be towed from the banks; and for dropping downstream with the current they are handled as follows: each vessel is equipped with a raft made of tamarisk wood, with a rush mat fastened on top of it, and a stone with a hole through it weighing some four hundredweight; the raft and the stone are made fast to the vessel with ropes, fore and aft respectively, so that the raft is carried rapidly forward by the current and pulls the "baris" (as these boats are called) after it, while the stone, dragging along the bottom astern, acts as a check and gives her steerage-way [keeps the raft and boat from drifting away]. There are a great many of these vessels on the Nile, some of them of enormous carrying capacity.[51]

Such craft were generally adequate for navigating the river; but scholars maintain that they were not strong and flexible enough to hold up in the open sea, especially carrying heavy loads. Therefore, the troop transports that crossed from the delta to the coast of Syria-Palestine under Sahura, Thutmose III, and others were reinforced. The most common means was adding trusses, heavy rope bindings wrapped tightly around the hull at various points.

The Coming of the Sea Peoples

It is unlikely that the warriors these ships transported were trained to fight at sea; and most had little or no skill in sailing the vessels. In fact, the navy, if it can be called that, was not yet a separate, formal branch of the military (and probably never became so); ships simply supported the land army when and where necessary. It is unclear when the Egyptian government began assembling and training crews specifically for naval warfare. What is certain is that by the reign of Rameses III, the country was able to muster a fleet of ships manned by such crews (although this naval force may have been a temporary rather than permanent measure). The normal complement of such a ship was fifty men, each trained as both sailor and marine. Evidence from reliefs indicates that under battle conditions twenty of the men operated the oars while the others fought with bows, javelins, and swords.

The natural question is why, after more than two thousand years with no trained naval arm, the Egyptian military saw fit to create one? The answer can only be that it suddenly perceived an urgent need for specialized sea fighters. And this is quite consistent with a dramatic series of events that affected not only Egypt but the entire eastern Mediterranean sphere in the thirteenth and twelfth centuries B.C.—an unexpected and catastrophic upheaval of unprecedented scope. The trouble seems to have begun far north of Egypt, in Asia Minor or beyond, and steadily spread southward. Nearly all of the leading towns and cities in Asia Minor were sacked, burned, and destroyed, most never to be rebuilt; among them were Hattusas and the other important Hittite centers, bringing about Hatti's sudden and utter collapse. Farther south, Ugarit and other prosperous Syrian and Palestinian coastal ports were also plundered and devastated.

At the same time, Egypt came under direct assault from the northwest and north.

THE CATASTROPHE CIRCA 1200 B.C.

Historians have advanced a number of theories to explain the widespread catastrophe that ravaged large sections of the eastern Mediterranean about 1200 B.C. and brought about the collapse of the Bronze Age in the region. Some think that rapid local population growth among the semibarbarous tribes inhabiting "Eurasia," the vast steppe lands north of the Black and Caspian Seas, caused them to migrate southward in search of new lands, destroying all in their path. The Mediterranean coastal peoples they displaced then became the Sea Peoples, who menaced the Egyptians. Another theory discounts the idea of mass migrations; it holds instead that a large portion of the destruction was caused by civil conflicts, economic collapse, and other crises within the eastern Mediterranean states themselves, which less civilized peoples on the periphery then took advantage of. And still another view, advanced recently by Robert Drews of Vanderbilt University, is that military innovations among these "periphery" peoples suddenly gave their foot soldiers the ability to defeat the chariot corps that had for centuries been the mainstay of Near Eastern armies. Among these proposed innovations were the new tactic of javelin throwers "swarming" chariots and their crews, thereby neutralizing them; the adoption of better protective armor by foot soldiers; and the introduction of new, deadly slashing swords. A detailed discussion of these theories appears in Drews's *The End of the Bronze Age: Changes in Warfare and the Catastrophe ca. 1200 B.C.*

The attacks, by groups of foreigners the Egyptians collectively called the Sea Peoples, came in waves, each apparently larger and more threatening than the one before it. A small foretaste came during the reign of Rameses II in the form of raids on the delta by Sherdan pirates. The pharaoh rather easily repelled these small-scale attacks and eventually incorporated some of the defeated Sherdan into the Egyptian army. Rameses also erected a row of fortresses along the northern coastline, hoping this would suffice to ward off any future assaults on that region.

Egypt would have been much better off if Rameses had constructed a permanent navy, for the scope of the threat turned out to be much greater than he imagined at the time. In the fifth year of the reign of his successor, Merneptah, about 1208 B.C., a force of Sea Peoples—with names like Shekelesh, Lukka, Tjeker, and Akawasha—allied themselves with the Libyans and invaded Egypt from the northwest. They brought their families and possessions with them, indicating that they intended to settle permanently in the country. But the pharaoh managed to defeat the intruders in a pitched battle near the western side of the delta; he claimed to have killed six thousand of them and captured another nine thousand.

During the short reigns of the five pharaohs who followed Merneptah, reports of devastation wrought elsewhere in the Near East by new waves of Sea Peoples must have filtered into Egypt. It is also quite possible that small-scale raids by foreigners continued periodically in the delta region.

These factors may well have inspired an Egyptian pharaoh, perhaps Rameses III himself, to invest in some kind of naval preparedness.

The Sea Battle in the Delta

Whoever was behind the Egyptian naval effort, it certainly paid off. In the tenth year of Rameses' reign (ca. 1176 B.C.), the largest invasion of Sea Peoples to date struck northern Egypt. This time the foreigners had a new ally in their midst—the Peleset, whom historians believe were the Philistines (who would later settle in Palestine and become the biblical enemies of the Hebrews). A first wave of invaders must have landed well to the west of the delta and marched overland; for Rameses met and defeated them in a land battle. Not long afterward, however, more Sea Peoples approached the delta in ships. A huge naval battle occurred, captured for posterity in a stunning stone relief in Rameses' mortuary temple at Medinat Habu (near Thebes). Scholar Manuel Robbins describes the scene, which reveals much about the naval tactics the Egyptians employed at the time:

A modern rendering of pharaoh Rameses III, who repulsed the invasion of the so-called Sea Peoples in the twelfth century B.C.

A detail of the complex depiction of the great sea battle with the Sea Peoples in a stone relief at Rameses' mortuary temple at Medinat Habu.

The Sea Battle sculptural relief on the north wall of the temple is about 55 feet wide and . . . was originally augmented with plaster and paint. Here, represented in a compressed composition . . . was a clash which occurred on the water somewhere near shore. . . . On the right stands the pharaoh . . . launching shafts at the enemy from his unerring bow. Stretching across the bottom of the illustration are Egyptian soldiers, marching off with Sea Peoples prisoners. On the left is the battle on the water. . . . Here there is a clash among ships . . . [which] are arranged in three rows, one above the other. In each row there are three ships. Three along the left and one on the lower right are manned by Egyptians, and the rest are those of the Sea Peoples. . . . Two of these Sea Peoples ships are manned by warriors who wear . . . feathered headgear . . . and two others by those in horned helmets. . . . The Sea Peoples came armed only with close-combat weapons—dirk [daggerlike] swords and a few lances—and that was a fatal mistake. The Egyptian forces . . . had not only close-combat weapons but stand-off weapons as well, their bows. . . . The scene shows a fierce mêlée of close combat. Egyptian

RAMESES VANQUISHES THE INVADERS

In this inscription from the sea battle relief sculpture at Medinat Habu (quoted in volume 4 of J.H. Breasted's Ancient Records of Egypt*), the pharaoh Rameses III is portrayed as an invincible hero beating back the invading Sea Peoples.*

Lo, the [peoples of the] northern countries [i.e., the homelands of the Sea Peoples], which are in their isles, are restless in their limbs; they infest the ways of the [Egyptian and other Near Eastern] harbor-mouths. Their nostrils and their hearts cease breathing breath, when his majesty goes forth like a storm-wind against them, fighting upon the strand like a warrior. . . . Terror of him penetrates into their limbs. Capsized and perishing in their places, their hearts are taken, their souls fly away, and their weapons are cast out upon the sea. His arrows pierce whomsoever he will among them, and he who is hit falls into the water. His majesty is like an enraged lion, tearing him that confronts him with his hands; fighting at close quarters on his right, valiant on his left, he has crushed every land beneath his feet.

boats have their oars out so that they are able to maneuver, but in the Sea Peoples boats, oars are shipped [pulled inside the vessels]. They are unable to maneuver. They have been caught by surprise it seems. From a crow's nest on an Egyptian ship, a slinger rains missiles down on the Sea Peoples. A grappling hook has been swung out from an Egyptian ship and lands on a Sea Peoples ship. The ship is hauled close and a Sea Peoples fighter is dispatched with a lance. Another Sea Peoples ship is dismasted, a third capsized. Sea Peoples are in disarray, drowned, dead. The water is filled with them.[52]

The illustrative portions of the relief are supplemented by inscriptions. Together, the pictures and words provide enough detail to allow historians to reconstruct the event—the first well-documented sea battle in history—with some confidence. The most striking aspect is that the invaders were trapped between the Egyptian ships and Egyptian archers and other infantry on the shore. Archers, both ground-based and on the Egyptian ships, poured arrows onto the enemy boats, killing many aboard and spreading terror and confusion. Then the Egyptian vessels moved in close and used grappling hooks to snag the enemy ships. Egyptian marines boarded and fought hand to hand; or in some cases they towed the boats close enough to shore that the infantry could seize and board them. Those Sea Peoples who were not killed in the fighting were dragged away as prisoners. One of the Medinat Habu inscriptions puts these words in Rameses' mouth:

Those who reached my boundary, their . . . heart and soul are finished forever and ever. As for those who had assembled before them on the sea, the full flame [i.e., the fleet of Egyptian warships] was in their front, before the harbor-mouths, and a wall of metal [the Egyptian infantrymen] upon the shore surrounded them. They [the invaders] ships' were dragged, overturned, and laid low upon the beach; [the wretched enemy were] slain and made [into] heaps from stern to bow of their galleys, while all their things were cast upon the water. [53]

Careful Planning Saves Egypt

What the reliefs and inscriptions unfortunately leave out is how the Egyptians were able to lure the enemy into the trap. The clever and precise positioning and coordination of the Egyptian naval and land forces could not have been a spontaneous development or fortunate accident. The trap and subsequent victory, which saved Egypt, were the result of careful planning. As in the battle at Kadesh, military intelligence must have played an important role. Either the pharaoh's spies, perhaps paid informants among the enemy forces, were able to pinpoint the area of the delta where the Sea Peoples planned to land; or the spies, or other parties working for the pharaoh convinced the invaders to land there, luring them into a trap.

Another possibility is that the pharaoh pretended to surrender without a fight. Perhaps he sent secret envoys to the leaders of the Sea Peoples to say that he feared them and had decided to submit rather than fight; they could land and settle in the delta without interference providing they spared him and allowed him to keep his throne. Such a plea was likely not without precedent. In their attacks on Near Eastern coasts, the Sea Peoples quite probably received many offers of submission from frightened local leaders. The difference in this case was that Rameses was neither frightened nor actually submitting. After the invaders had taken the bait, he sprang his trap and annihilated them.

It may never be possible to know exactly how the Egyptians trapped their opponents. What is certain is that Rameses' victory, though important to Egypt in the short run, was a mere stopgap measure in the long term. Some of the surviving Sea Peoples, particularly the Peleset and Tjeker, settled in Palestine, the last remnant of Egypt's once large Asiatic sphere of influence. Soon these settlers took control of the region, shutting the Egyptians out. By the reign of the last New Kingdom pharaoh (Rameses XI, 1099–1069 B.C.), Egyptian ships were no longer able to get regular supplies of cedar wood and other products from the area. Egypt's military and political might had clearly passed their prime, and in the centuries to follow their decline would continue.

Decline of the Egyptian Military

E gypt's political strength during most of the New Kingdom, both internally as a country united under a single ruler and externally as a great international power, had been largely based on its successful military ventures in Syria-Palestine. When the country's influence in that region began to wane, so did its military and political fortunes. During the two historical eras that followed the New Kingdom—the Third Intermediate Period (1069–747 B.C.) and Late Period (747–332 B.C.)—the military and the profession of soldiering lost the prestigious status they had held for several centuries. As a result, local rulers increasingly relied on foreign mercenaries to man the army ranks; Egypt steadily became a second-rate, even a third-rate power; and eventually a series of foreign rulers came to dominate the country, among them Assyrians, Persians, Greeks, and Romans.

An Emphasis on Paid Soldiers

Several reasons can be cited for Egypt's military and political decline. Among the most telling was an inability to keep up with material and technological changes occurring across most of the Near Eastern and Mediterranean spheres. In particular, iron tools and weapons began to replace bronze versions; and armies equipped with iron swords and spearheads had a distinct advantage on the battlefield. The problem for Egypt was that it had no native supplies of iron. That metal had to be imported, mainly from western Asia; but by the start of the Third Intermediate Period, the country's influence and trade contacts in that area were at a low ebb.

Even more problematic was a growing tendency to leave the army and military matters in the hands of foreigners rather than native Egyptians. Nubians, Libyans, Sherdan, and others had long been recruited to fight as ethnic units in the army, of course. Similarly, in the years following the defeat of the Sea Peoples by Rameses III, he and the later Ramesside rulers allowed some of the remnants of the Sea Peoples to settle in Egypt and recruited them into the

86

army. For the most part, following custom, these groups were commanded by Egyptians and adequately controlled by the state.

But as major military expeditions and glorious conquests became a thing of the past, fewer and fewer native Egyptians became interested in military service; consequently, the foreign units within the army became dominant, while the government increasingly hired mercenaries to supplement their ranks. In the early years of the Third Intermediate Period, as Sheikh 'Ibada al-Nubi explains,

imported Libyan mercenaries . . . were led by their own princes. They did not adopt Egyptian names, as foreigners who had acquired importance in the past had done. They wore an ostrich feather, the characteristic decoration of their people, proudly on their heads. Distributed throughout the country in garrisons reserved for them, their generals assumed more power as the [central power of the] monarchy and the administration became increasingly

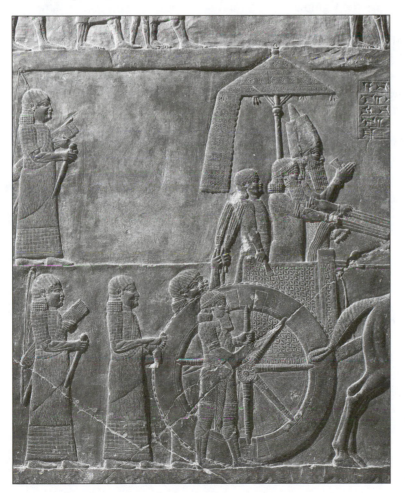

King Assurbanipal was the second Assyrian ruler to control Egypt. He defeated Taharqo, the reigning pharaoh, who fled southward to Thebes.

uncertain. They became princes and official priests of the local gods, effectively taking over the king's prerogatives [exclusive powers and privileges]. Finally, one of their number, Sheshonq I, ascended the throne, initiating what is known as the "Libyan" dynasty. [54]

Even before the advent of the Libyan dynasty (945–715 B.C.), the country had become politically fragmented. Throughout the Third Intermediate Period, two major power bases claimed to have the legitimate pharaoh—one in the Nile Delta, the other in Thebes. And at various times, individual cities asserted local independence and power. The military was similarly fragmented, with local princes commanding their own small armies, which sometimes fought one another.

No Match for the Assyrian Army

The situation changed somewhat at the start of the Late Period (747 B.C.), when a dynasty of Nubian kings pushed their way north and took control of much of Lower Egypt. The country was still not completely reunified, as several local rulers still held their own against the new pharaohs. But the Nubian kings gained enough power and confidence to attempt something bold— to reassert Egyptian influence in Syria-Palestine. Unfortunately for them, by this time the Assyrian Empire had grown very strong and begun to intrude into the same region. So the new Egyptian foray into Palestine came to nothing.

Worse still, the warlike Assyrians saw that the Egyptian army was no match for

their own. In 674 B.C. an Assyrian king, Esarhaddon, invaded Egypt and managed to subdue the capital, then at Memphis, and most of the countryside surrounding it in less than a month. "Without cessation I slew multitudes of his men," Esarhaddon later said about the Egyptian king, Taharqo.

Memphis, his royal city, in half a day, with mines, tunnels, assaults, I besieged, I captured . . . I burned with fire. His queen, his harem, his . . . sons and daughters, his property and his goods, his horses, his cattle, his sheep, in countless numbers, I carried off to Assyria. [55]

Despite this initial success, Esarhaddon found it difficult to maintain control over the proud Egyptians. Two years after the departure of the main Assyrian army, Taharqo, who had fled far to the south, returned, recaptured Memphis, and staged a full-scale rebellion. While on his way back to Egypt to quell this disturbance, Esarhaddon died unexpectedly and his son, the crown prince Assurbanipal, succeeded him. Assurbanipal made his way through Syria-Palestine and entered Egypt, where, according to his annals:

Taharqo, king of Egypt . . . heard of the advance of my army, in Memphis, and mustered his fighting men against me, offering armed resistance and battle. With the help of Assur . . . [and other Assyrian] gods . . . who advanced at my side, I defeated his army in a battle on the open plain. . . . He forsook Memphis and fled to Thebes. [56]

ASSYRIAN MILITARY ADVANCES

Many of the weapons of the formidable Assyrian army that invaded Egypt were similar to those used in the late second millennium B.C., although some of the tactics had changed. The principal Assyrian weapon was the bow, most often utilized in the main tactical field unit—the archer pair. This consisted of two men, the first a spear- or dagger-man bearing a very large shield, the top of which curved up and back to form a kind of canopy to protect against incoming arrows and other missiles. Made of tightly packed bundles of wicker bound with leather, such shields were light but very sturdy. The second man, the archer, who huddled with his companion behind the shield, used a powerful composite bow to fire off volleys of arrows. Rows of hundreds or thousands of these pairs, who in battle moved forward in unison, made up the mainstay of the Assyrian infantry. Assyrian chariots featured a similar arrangement—a driver and archer standing behind a protective screen mounted on the vehicle's front. However, by this time chariots had become secondary to cavalry, which at first, like the infantry, operated in two-man units. Ancient Assyrian reliefs show two horsemen galloping along together. One holds the reins of both his own and his partner's horse, allowing the partner to use both hands to fire a bow. If one rider's horse was killed or injured, he could quickly jump on his partner's horse and ride to safety.

When the Assyrians pursued Taharqo to Thebes, he fled again and died in exile. Others then took up the cause of Egyptian independence, including his son, Tanuatamun, and the leader of a new dynasty, Psamtek I. Eventually, a rebellion in Babylonia forced the Assyrians to call most of their forces home, after which Psamtek succeeded in driving the remaining Assyrian occupiers out of the country. A patriotic, well-meaning ruler, Psamtek realized he needed a strong army to keep the Assyrians and other invaders at bay. Instead of re-creating a military institution manned and commanded mainly by native Egyptians, however, he cast his net wide for foreign mercenaries. In particular, he hired Greeks, mostly from western Asia Minor. This marked the beginning of Egypt's political dealings with and eventual absorption into the classical Greco-Roman world.

Persians, Greeks, and Romans

Using these Greek mercenaries, the Egyptians tried to maintain their independence from greater powers that rose and fell around them, but to no avail. In the late 500s B.C., the Persian Empire, which had supplanted the Assyrian realm, conquered both Egypt and its main source of military recruits, the Greek cities of Asia Minor. Persian rule was so unpopular in Egypt that when Alexander III (later called "the Great"), a Macedonian-Greek king, entered the country in 332 B.C. as part of his conquest of Persia, he was welcomed as a liberator. This was an illusion, however. Alexander soon died and one of his leading generals, Ptolemy, took control of

Egypt and established a Greek dynasty—the Ptolemaic (332–30 B.C.).

Under the Ptolemies, Egypt became part of the greater Greek world that now encompassed the entire eastern Mediterranean sphere. To defend against other Greek kingdoms, the government maintained a strong military. At first it was made up mainly of imported Greek mercenaries, as before; but over time the Ptolemaic kings saw the wisdom of supplementing paid soldiers with native-born troops, thereby reestablishing a new prestigious military institution.

The problem was that the vast majority of officers at most levels remained Greeks, who were natives merely by virtue of their parents or grandparents having settled in the country. The status of ethnic Egyptians was inferior to Greeks, both in the army ranks and in society as a whole. (Some modern scholars have used the analogy of the authority and paternalism of British officers over native soldiers and citizens in India in the 1800s and early 1900s.)

These military and social distinctions became a moot point in the long run, though. As time went on, Ptolemaic Egypt became militarily and politically impotent in the face of Rome's rise to dominance over the entire Mediterranean world. And by the first century B.C., Rome had conquered all the Greek states except for Egypt, which more or less cowered in its shadow.

A bust of Alexander III (later called "the Great"), the young Macedonian Greek king who liberated Egypt from the Persians in the late fourth century B.C.

A seventeenth-century engraving of the battle of Actium, in which Julius Caesar's adopted son, Octavian, defeated Cleopatra, the last independent ruler of Egypt.

Then the last of the Ptolemies, as well as the last independent Egyptian pharaoh—Cleopatra VII—made a bold eleventh-hour bid to reassert her country's former greatness. Allying herself with a powerful Roman, Mark Antony, she opposed his rival, Octavian, in a Roman civil war. In 31 B.C., however, she and Antony went down to defeat in a large naval battle at Actium, in Greece; and the following year Cleopatra and Antony committed suicide. To the displeasure of most Egyptians, Octavian proceeded to make Egypt a province of Rome. And so it was that the military establishment of an independent Egypt, whose proud traditions stretched back with only a few brief interruptions for more than three millennia, now simply ceased to exist.

Notes

Introduction: Fighting to Keep the Dark Forces at Bay

1. Sheikh 'Ibada al-Nubi, "Soldiers," in Sergio Donadoni, ed., *The Egyptians,* trans. Robert Bianchi et al. Chicago: University of Chicago Press, 1990, p. 151.
2. Quoted in Miriam Lichtheim, ed., *Ancient Egyptian Literature: A Book of Readings.* Berkeley: University of California Press, 1975–1976, vol. 1, pp. 103–104.
3. al-Nubi, in Donadoni, *Egyptians,* p. 152.
4. Quoted in James B. Pritchard, ed., *Ancient Near Eastern Texts Relating to the Old Testament.* Princeton: Princeton University Press, 1969, p. 262.

Chapter One: Early Egyptian Weapons and Warfare

5. Andrea M. Gnirs, "Ancient Egypt," in Kurt Raaflaub and Nathan Rosenstein, eds., *War and Society in the Ancient and Medieval Worlds.* Cambridge, MA: Harvard University Press, 1999, p. 78.
6. Quoted in Pritchard, *Ancient Near Eastern Texts,* p. 228.
7. Yigael Yadin, *The Art of Warfare in Biblical Lands in the Light of Archaeological Study.* New York: McGraw-Hill, 1963, vol. 1, p. 44.
8. Ian Shaw, *Egyptian Warfare and Weapons.* Buckinghamshire, UK: Shire Publications, 1991, pp. 36–37.
9. Shaw, *Egyptian Warfare and Weapons,* p. 25.
10. al-Nubi, in Donadoni, *Egyptians,* p. 158.
11. Quoted in W.K. Simpson, ed., *The Literature of Ancient Egypt: An Anthology of Stories, Instructions, and Poetry.* New Haven: Yale University Press, 1973, pp. 61–62.
12. Yadin, *Art of Warfare,* vol. 1, p. 73.

Chapter Two: The New Kingdom and Chariot Warfare

13. Quoted in J.H. Breasted, ed., *Ancient Records of Egypt.* New York: Russell and Russell, 1962, vol. 2, pp. 6–7.
14. Mark Healy, *Armies of the Pharaohs.* Oxford: Osprey, 1992, pp. 9–10.
15. Quoted in Breasted, *Ancient Records,* vol. 2, p. 30.
16. Quoted in Breasted, *Ancient Records,* vol. 2, p. 34.
17. Yadin, *Art of Warfare,* vol. 1, pp. 86–87.
18. Gnirs, "Ancient Egypt," in Raaflaub and Rosenstein, *War and Society,* p. 85.
19. Quoted in Shaw, *Egyptian Warfare and Weapons,* pp. 41–42.

20. Healy, *Armies of the Pharaohs*, p. 21.
21. Robert Drews, *The End of the Bronze Age: Changes in Warfare and the Catastrophe ca. 1200 B.C.* Princeton: Princeton University Press, 1993, pp. 127–29.
22. Quoted in Breasted, *Ancient Records,* vol. 2, p. 183.
23. Quoted in Breasted, *Ancient Records,* vol. 2, p. 184.
24. Quoted in Breasted, *Ancient Records,* vol. 2, pp. 184–85.

Chapter Three: Military Service and Organization
25. al-Nubi, in Donadoni, *Egyptians,* pp. 171–72.
26. Healy, *Armies of the Pharaohs,* p. 17.
27. Healy, *Armies of the Pharaohs,* p. 24.
28. Quoted in Alan R. Shulman, *Military Rank, Title and Organization in the Egyptian New Kingdom.* Berlin: Verlag Bruno Hessling, 1964, p. 108.
29. Shulman, *Military Rank,* pp. 23–24.
30. Quoted in Breasted, *Ancient Records,* vol. 3, pp. 52–53.
31. Quoted in Shulman, *Military Rank,* p. 108.
32. Quoted in Breasted, *Ancient Records,* vol. 3, p. 27.
33. Quoted in Breasted, *Ancient Records,* vol. 3, pp. 27–28.
34. Quoted in Breasted, *Ancient Records,* vol. 3, p. 28.
35. al-Nubi, in Donadoni, *Egyptians,* p. 178.

Chapter Four: Borders, Fortifications, and Sieges
36. Peter Connolly, *Greece and Rome at War.* London: Greenhill Books, 1998, p. 274.
37. Quoted in Breasted, *Ancient Records,* vol. 1, pp. 293–94.
38. Yadin, *Art of Warfare,* vol. 1, p. 66.
39. Quoted in Breasted, *Ancient Records,* vol. 2, pp. 185–86.
40. Deuteronomy 20:19–20.
41. Yadin, *Art of Warfare,* vol. 1, p. 97.
42. Quoted in Yadin, *Art of Warfare,* vol. 1, p. 99.

Chapter Five: Egypt's Military Zenith: The Battle of Kadesh
43. Mark Healy, *The Warrior Pharaoh: Rameses II and the Battle of Qadesh.* Oxford: Osprey, 1993, p. 9.
44. Quoted in Breasted, *Ancient Records,* vol. 3, p. 72.
45. Some scholars speculate variously that these fighters consisted of part or all of the army unit of Seth, or that they were a crack force of Palestinian soldiers who fought as an ethnic unit in the Egyptian army.
46. Breasted, *Ancient Records,* vol. 3, pp. 129–31.
47. Quoted in Breasted, *Ancient Records,* vol. 3, p. 144.
48. Quoted in Breasted, *Ancient Records,* vol. 3, p. 146.
49. Healy, *Warrior Pharaoh,* p. 53.

Chapter Six: Warships and the Defeat of the Sea Peoples
50. Björn Landström, *Ships of the Pharaohs: 4000 Years of Egyptian*

Shipbuilding. Garden City, NY: Doubleday, 1970, p. 108.

51. Herodotus, *Histories,* trans. Aubrey de Sélincourt. New York: Penguin, 1972, pp. 164–65.

52. Manuel Robbins, *The Collapse of the Bronze Age: The Story of Greece, Troy, Israel, Egypt, and the Peoples of the Sea.* San Jose: Authors Choice Press, 2001, pp. 284–86.

53. Quoted in Breasted, *Ancient Records,* vol. 4, p. 39.

Epilogue: Decline of the Egyptian Military

54. al-Nubi, in Donadoni, *Egyptians,* p. 180.

55. Quoted in Daniel D. Luckenbill, ed., *Ancient Records of Assyria and Babylonia.* Chicago: University of Chicago Press, 1926. Reprint, New York: Greenwood Press, 1968, vol. 2, p. 227.

56. Quoted in Luckenbill, *Ancient Records,* vol. 2, p. 293.

Glossary

archaeology: The study of past civilizations and their artifacts.

bronze: An alloy (mixture) of the metals copper and tin.

composite bow: A bow made by gluing together pieces of wood, animal sinew, and horn; composite bows had greater elasticity and range than ordinary "simple" bows.

crenellation: The notched effect in the battlements of forts, castles, and other ancient and medieval structures; the notches, which the defenders used for protection, are called merlons; the openings between them, through which they fired at attackers, are the crenels.

dynasty: A series of rulers belonging to one family line.

Egyptology: The branch of archaeology dealing specifically with ancient Egypt.

electrum: An alloy of gold and silver.

epsilon ax: A Near Eastern battle-ax having three tangs projecting from the back of the blade, giving it a shape that roughly resembled the Greek letter epsilon.

grappling hooks: Devices thrown or shot onto enemy ships to hold them fast and pull them closer, often so that fighters can board the other ships and fight hand to hand.

inscriptions: Letters and words carved into stone or some other durable material.

intelligence: In the military context, information gathered by one side about the size, quality, movements, and/or plans of the other.

javelin: A throwing spear.

khopesh: A short, sickle-shaped sword introduced into Egypt near the beginning of the New Kingdom.

mace: A club used in warfare.

pharaoh: The king of ancient Egypt.

relief: A stone sculpture partly raised into three dimensions from a flat surface.

scribe: In the Egyptian military, an officer in charge of keeping track of men and materials, distributing supplies, and other administrative tasks.

standard: The symbol of an army or army unit, usually carried into battle by a standard-bearer.

tst: A term describing a large army unit during the Old Kingdom.

vizier: A high nonmilitary official who administered the kingdom for the pharaoh.

yoke: A device for attaching a horse's harness to a chariot or wagon.

For Further Reading

George Hart, *Ancient Egypt*. New York: Time-Life, 1995. A very colorfully illustrated introduction to the wonders of ancient Egypt for young readers.

Hazel M. Martell, *The Ancient World: From the Ice Age to the Fall of Rome*. New York: Kingfisher, 1995. A very handsomely mounted book that briefly examines the various important ancient civilizations, including ancient Egypt.

Anne Millard, *Mysteries of the Pyramids*. Brookfield, CT: Copper Beach Books, 1995. Aimed at basic readers, this book by a noted scholar is short but brightly illustrated and filled with interesting facts about the pyramids and ancient Egyptian life.

Neil Morris, *Atlas of Ancient Egypt*. New York: NTC Contemporary Publishing, 2000. This excellent book about ancient Egypt contains many maps and also several impressive double-page spreads of specific eras and aspects of everyday life. Highly recommended.

David Murdock, *Tutankhamun: The Life and Death of a Pharaoh*. London: Dorling Kindersley, 1998. A beautifully illustrated examination of an Egyptian ruler who died young and was later forgotten, only to become famous in modern times when scholars unearthed his tomb.

Don Nardo, *Ancient Egypt*. San Diego: KidHaven Press, 2002. A general overview of Egyptian civilization, with an emphasis on history, aimed at basic readers.

———, *Egyptian Mythology*. Berkeley Heights, NJ: Enslow, 2001. Aimed at intermediate readers, this book retells some of the most famous Egyptian myths, including the story of Osiris's murder by Seth.

———, *Pyramids of Egypt*. New York: Franklin Watts, 2002. Tells when, how, and by whom the pyramids were built, supported by many beautiful pictures. The target audience is grade school readers.

Don Nardo, ed., *Cleopatra*. San Diego: Greenhaven Press, 2001. The reading level of this volume is challenging for grade school students but well worth the effort. In a series of short essays, noted scholars tell nearly all that is known about this famous queen and her exploits.

Kelly Trumble, *Cat Mummies*. Boston: Houghton Mifflin, 1999. An unusual and nicely illustrated volume that tells why cats were important in ancient Egyptian society and how these animals were mummified.

Major Works Consulted

Modern Sources

Sergio Donadoni, ed., *The Egyptians.* Trans. Robert Bianchi et al. Chicago: University of Chicago Press, 1990. This excellent collection of authoritative essays about ancient Egypt has a long, detailed, insightful tract about Egyptian warfare by noted Middle Eastern scholar Sheikh 'Ibada al-Nubi.

Robert Drews, *The End of the Bronze Age: Changes in Warfare and the Catastrophe ca. 1200 B.C.* Princeton: Princeton University Press, 1993. The best available general overview of Bronze Age warfare. Drews also summarizes the various theories for why many Greek and Near Eastern kingdoms collapsed in the period in question. Highly recommended.

Nicolas Grimal, *A History of Ancient Egypt.* Trans. Ian Shaw. Oxford: Blackwell, 1992. An outstanding scholarly study of ancient Egyptian history.

Sir John Hackett, ed., *Warfare in the Ancient World.* New York: Facts On File, 1989. This extremely informative and handsome volume is a collection of long, detailed essays by world-class historians, each of whom tackles the military development and methods of a single ancient people or empire. The beautiful and accurate illustrations are by the famous scholar-artist Peter Connolly. Of main interest for the purposes of this volume on Egyptian warfare is "The Beginnings of Warfare" by Dr. Trevor Watkins, of the archaeology department at Edinburgh University, who summarizes the weapons and tactics of various Near Eastern peoples.

Mark Healy, *Armies of the Pharaohs.* Oxford: Osprey, 1992. Beautifully illustrated, like other books in the Osprey military series, this one begins with the ejection of the Hyksos and inauguration of the New Kingdom and covers the major aspects of the Egyptian military in a straightforward, easy-to-read manner.

———, *The Warrior Pharaoh: Rameses II and the Battle of Qadesh.* Oxford:

Osprey, 1993. In general terms, this volume covers some of the same ground as Healy's other book on the Egyptian army (see above) but goes into voluminous detail about the confrontation at Qadesh (or Kadesh). This is the most detailed nonscholarly look at this pivotal battle since J.H. Breasted's 1903 classic on the topic (see Additional Works Consulted).

Björn Landström, *Ships of the Pharaohs: 4000 Years of Egyptian Shipbuilding.* Garden City, NY: Doubleday, 1970. A very thorough, extremely well-illustrated description of ancient Egyptian ships, including warships. Highly recommended for those interested in ancient nautical lore.

Kurt Raaflaub and Nathan Rosenstein, eds., *War and Society in the Ancient and Medieval Worlds.* Cambridge, MA: Harvard University Press, 1999. An excellent collection of essays by noted historians, each summarizing the basic methods of warfare utilized by an ancient people. The selection on Egyptian warfare is by Andrea M. Gnirs.

Donald B. Redford, *Egypt, Canaan, and Israel in Ancient Times.* Princeton: Princeton University Press, 1992. This useful study covers, among other things, the Egyptian military expeditions into Palestine and their political consequences.

Nancy K. Sanders, *The Sea Peoples: Warriors of the Ancient Mediterranean, 1250–1150 B.C.* London: Thames and Hudson, 1985. A thoughtful discussion of the mass population movements and invasions that brought various peoples of southern Europe and the northern Near East into collision with the Egyptians near the close of the New Kingdom.

Ian Shaw, *Egyptian Warfare and Weapons.* Buckinghamshire, UK: Shire Publications, 1991. A brief but highly informative overview of the subject, presented in a format and language suitable for students and general readers.

Alan R. Shulman, *Military Rank, Title, and Organization in the Egyptian New Kingdom.* Berlin: Verlag Bruno Hessling, 1964. Distributed in the United States by Argonaut Publishers, Chicago. A scholarly examination of ancient Egyptian army officers and soldiers, supplemented by numerous primary source quotations.

Yigael Yadin, *The Art of Warfare in Biblical Lands in the Light of Archaeological Study.* 2 vols. New York: McGraw-Hill, 1963. A very large, comprehensive, and well-illustrated study of ancient weapons and warfare in Palestine and neighboring lands, including a great deal on the Egyptian military. The text is supported by numerous photos of archaeological sites and artifacts. Highly recommended.

Ancient Sources

J.H. Breasted, ed., *Ancient Records of Egypt.* 5 vols. New York: Russell and Russell, 1962.

Herodotus, *Histories.* Trans. Aubrey de Sélincourt. New York: Penguin, 1972.

Holy Bible. Revised Standard Version. New York: Thomas Nelson and Sons, 1952.

Miriam Lichtheim, ed., *Ancient Egyptian Literature: A Book of Readings.* 2 vols. Berkeley: University of California Press, 1975–1976.

Daniel D. Luckenbill, ed., *Ancient Records of Assyria and Babylonia.* 2 vols. Chicago: University of Chicago Press, 1926. Reprint, New York: Greenwood Press, 1968.

James B. Pritchard, ed., *Ancient Near Eastern Texts Relating to the Old Testament.* Princeton: Princeton University Press, 1969.

W.K. Simpson, ed., *The Literature of Ancient Egypt: An Anthology of Stories, Instructions, and Poetry.* New Haven: Yale University Press, 1973.

Additional Works
Consulted

William Y. Adams, *Nubia: Corridor to Africa.* London: Penguin, 1977.

Paul G. Bahn, ed., *The Cambridge Illustrated History of Archaeology.* New York: Cambridge University Press, 1996.

J.H. Breasted, *The Battle of Kadesh: A Study in the Earliest Known Military Strategy.* Chicago: Oriental Institute, 1903.

Lionel Casson, *Ancient Egypt.* New York: Time-Life, 1965.

Peter Connolly, *Greece and Rome at War.* London: Greenhill Books, 1998.

Silvio Curto, *The Military Art of the Ancient Egyptians.* Turin, Italy: Fratelli Pozzo, 1971.

R.O. Faulkner, "The Battle of Megiddo," *Journal of Egyptian Archaeology,* vol. 28, 1942.

———, "Egyptian Military Organization," *Journal of Egyptian Archaeology,* vol. 39, 1953.

———, "Egyptian Seagoing Ships," *Journal of Egyptian Archaeology,* vol. 26, 1940.

Charles Freeman, *Egypt, Greece, and Rome: Civilizations of the Ancient Mediterranean.* New York: Oxford University Press, 1996.

Roberta L. Harris, *The World of the Bible.* London: Thames and Hudson, 1995.

Michael A. Hoffman, *Egypt Before the Pharaohs: The Prehistoric Foundations of Egyptian Civilization.* Austin: University of Texas Press, 1991.

John Keegan, *A History of Warfare.* New York: Random House, 1993.

A.W. Lawrence, "Ancient Egyptian Fortifications," *Journal of Egyptian Archaeology,* vol. 51, 1955.

A. Lucas and J.R. Harris, *Ancient Egyptian Materials and Industries.* Mineola, NY: Dover Publications, 1999.

Roland A. Oliver, *Africa in the Iron Age, ca. 500 B.C. to A.D. 1400.* New York: Cambridge University Press, 1975.

Graham Philip, *Metal Weapons of the Early and Middle Bronze Ages in Syria-Palestine.* 2 vols. Oxford: B.A.R. International Series, 1989.

Manuel Robbins, *The Collapse of the Bronze Age: The Story of Greece, Troy, Israel, Egypt, and the Peoples of the Sea.* San Jose: Authors Choice Press, 2001.

Ian Shaw and Paul Nicholson, *The Dictionary of Ancient Egypt*. New York: Harry N. Abrams, 1995.

David P. Silverman, ed., *Ancient Egypt*. New York: Oxford University Press, 1997.

H.W.F. Saggs, *Civilization Before Greece and Rome*. New Haven: Yale University Press, 1989.

Alan R. Shulman, "Chariots, Chariotry, and the Hyksos," *Journal of the Society for the Study of Egyptian Antiquities,* vol. 10, 1979.

Wolfram von Soden, *The Ancient Orient: An Introduction to the Study of the Ancient Near East*. Trans. Donald G. Schley. Grand Rapids, MI: William B. Eerdmans, 1994.

Anthony J. Spalinger, *Aspects of the Military Documents of the Ancient Egyptians*. New Haven: Yale University Press, 1982.

Chester G. Starr, *A History of the Ancient World*. New York: Oxford University Press, 1991.

John Warry, *Warfare in the Classical World*. Norman: University of Oklahoma Press, 1995.

Index

Picture Credits

About the Author

Historian and award-winning writer Don Nardo has written or edited numerous books about the ancient world, including *Life in Ancient Athens, Greek and Roman Sport,* and *The Greenhaven Encyclopedia of Ancient Rome.* His studies of ancient and modern warfare include volumes on Greece, Rome, medieval times, the Revolutionary War, the War of 1812, the Mexican-American War, and World War II in the Pacific. Mr. Nardo lives with his wife, Christine, in Massachusetts.